The Boy Behind the Mask

The Boy Behind the Mask

MEETING THE REAL TUTANKHAMUN

Charlotte Booth

ONEWORLD
OXFORD

A Oneworld Book

Published by Oneworld Publications 2007
Copyright © Charlotte Booth 2007

ISBN-13: 978–1–85168–544–8
Typeset by Jayvee, Trivandrum, India
Cover design by D. R. Ink
Printed and bound by TJ International Ltd,
Padstow, Cornwall

Oneworld Publications
185 Banbury Road

Learn more about Oneworld. Join our mailing list to
find out about our latest titles and special offers at:

www.oneworld-publications.com

CONTENTS

ILLUSTRATIONS

PLATES

TIME LINE

Predynastic Period

The Badarian period – 4400–4000 BCE
Maadian period – 4000–3300 BCE
The Amratian period – 4000–3500 BCE
The Gerzean period – 3500–3200 BCE
The Negada III period – 3200–3050 BCE

Early Dynastic Period

Dynasty O – 3150–3050 BCE
Dynasty 1–3050–2890 BCE
Dynasty 2–2890–2686 BCE

Old Kingdom

Dynasty 3–2686–2613 BCE
Dynasty 4–2613–2500 BCE
Dynasty 5–2498–2345 BCE
Dynasty 6–2345–2333 BCE

First Intermediate Period

Dynasty 7 & 8–2180–2160 BCE
Dynasty 9 & 10–2160–2040 BCE

Middle Kingdom

Dynasty 11–2134–1991 BCE
Dynasty 12–1991–1782 BCE

Second Intermediate Period

Dynasty 13–1782–1650 BCE
Dynasty 14–?
Dynasty 15–1663–1555 BCE
Dynasty 16–1663–1555 BCE
Dynasty 17–1663–1570 BCE

New Kingdom

Dynasty 18–1570–1293 BCE
Dynasty 19–1293–1185 BCE
Dynasty 20–1185–1070 BCE

Third Intermediate Period

High Priests (Thebes) – 1080–945 BCE
Dynasty 21 (Tanis) – 1069–945 BCE
Dynasty 22 (Tanis) – 945–715 BCE
Dynasty 23 (Leontopolis) – 818–715 BCE
Dynasty 24 (Sais) – 727–715 BCE
Dynasty 25 (Nubians) – 747–656 BCE
Dynasty 26 (Sais) – 664–525 BCE

Late Period

Dynasty 27 (Persian) – 525–404 BCE
Dynasty 28–404–399 BCE
Dynasty 29–399–380 BCE
Dynasty 30–380–343 BCE
Dynasty 31–343–332 BCE

Graeco-Roman Period

Macedonian Kings – 332–305 BCE
Ptolemaic Period – 305–30 BCE

Reign of Akhenaten

Year 1–3 1350–47 BCE. Start of the co-regency with Amenhotep III. Year 1 of Akhenaten corresponds with year 27 of his father. A shrine is erected at Karnak dedicated to the Aten. Many of the traditional gods were still being represented at this time.

Year 4 1346 BCE. Work had started on the boundaries of the new capital at Akhetaten. The high priest of Amun is still active in quarrying expeditions. Third *heb sed* of Amenhotep III (year 30–1) and first of Amenhotep IV.

Year 5 1345 BCE. Amenhotep IV changed his name to Akhenaten. Princess Beketaten born, probably to Amenhotep III and Queen Tiye. Neferneferuaten was added to Nefertiti's name. Deliveries of wine started to Akhetaten. First representation of Princess Meritaten. Ankhesenepaten is born.

Year 6 1344 BCE. Akhenaten took up residence in his new city. Amun's temples in the Delta provided wine supply to the new city.

Year 7 1343 BCE. Tutankhaten was born at Amarna.

Year 8 1342 BCE. Princess Neferneferuaten is born.

Year 9 1341 BCE. The entire royal court moves to Akhetaten. All of the traditional temples are closed and Princess Neferneferure is born.

Year 10 1340 BCE. Amenhotep III paid his son a visit at Amarna and left a stela there.

Year 12 1338 BCE. Amenhotep III may have died (year 38). Tadukhipa arrives at the royal harem of Akhenaten.

Year 13 1337 BCE. Name of Nefertiti disappears from the monuments. Ankheperure Neferneferuaten co-rules with Akhenaten and is thought could be Nefertiti.

Year 14   1336 BCE. Princess Meketaten and Queen Tiye died. Smenkhkare became co-ruler with Akhenaten.

Year 15   1335 BCE. Ankhesenepaten marries Akhenaten (her father).

Year 17/1 1333 BCE. Akhenaten dies and Smenkhkare is the sole ruler for a short period, maybe only a few months. Ankhesenepaten marries Smenkhkare.

Reign of Tutankhamun

Year 1   1333 BCE. Tutankhamun marries Smenkhkare's widow, Ankhesenepaten.

Year 3   1331 BCE. Royal court transferred from Akhetaten to Memphis.

Year 4   1330 BCE: Tunic sent to Tutankhamun from Mitannian king?

Year 8   1326 BCE. Tutankhamun raises the taxes to pay for the restoration of the religious cults of Egypt.

Year 10   1324 BCE. Tutankhamun dies. His widow Ankhesenamun marries Ay.

FAMILY TREE

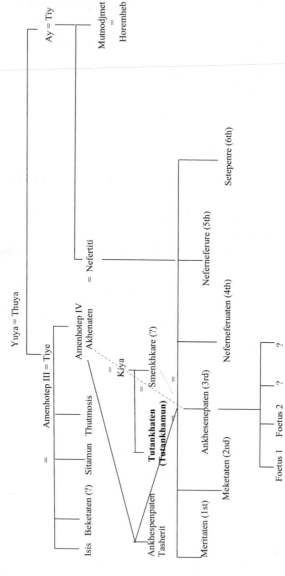

There are many unknowns in the family of Tutankhamun, and this family tree reflects the widely accepted theories, and the ones adopted throughout this book.

Introduction

The idea for this book developed from a study-day on Tutankhamun that I gave in Spring 2006. When I agreed to do it, I was filled with excitement. I suspected the audience were expecting a slide show of artefacts from his tomb and I wanted to present something completely different. I decided to do what no one else seemed to have done: to re-create the *life* of Tutankhamun, rather than focus on the treasures from his tomb and his death. While researching, I was surprised at how little there was on the life of this enigmatic king; even books entitled *The life of ...* seemed to focus purely on the tomb or were elaborate but general accounts of the eighteenth dynasty that focused on the life of Akhenaten, not Tutankhamun. This made the research difficult but all the more interesting and rewarding. At the end of the study day, I received nothing but positive feedback. Many people realised they knew very little about Tutankhamun, despite his world-wide fame and their familiarity with the treasures from his tomb. Later, I had an informal meeting with Marsha Filion of Oneworld Publications. We talked about books that need to be written and the Tutankhamun idea was raised. She persuaded me to write this book. The research has led to some very interesting discoveries, which I hope will shed light on the short but remarkable life of Tutankhamun.

Tutankhamun is one of the most famous kings of ancient Egypt, due to Howard Carter's 1922 discovery of his almost un-plundered tomb. However, although his tomb put his name in the history books, Tutankhamun was a relatively unimportant king, who ruled at the end of the Amarna period of the eighteenth dynasty. He was only a child when he came to the throne and died before he had reached full adulthood, perhaps at only eighteen or nineteen years old. Many kings achieved more and lived longer than Tutankhamun: for example, Pepy II, who ruled for ninety-four years in the Old Kingdom (2278–2184 BCE) and Thutmosis III, the first empire builder of the eighteenth dynasty (1504–1450 BCE). These kings are often pushed aside in favour of the glorious treasures in the tomb of this rather insignificant ruler.

Donald Redford, in his work on Akhenaten, commented on the reception of Tutankhamun by the western world:

> The unbelievable richness of his undisturbed tomb has so daz-zled us that it is hard to think of him as a human being. It has so distorted our vision that some of us are prepared to believe any-thing about the man ... a problem drinker, or one able to impose a curse on violation of his tomb. Let it be said once and for all that such notions, by whomsoever voiced, or undeservedly honoured by whatever screed, are unadulterated clap trap with no support at all in the meagre evidence we possess.[1]

Although somewhat abrupt, this statement is astute, as there has been constant speculation about the life of Tutankhamun since the discovery of his tomb. Theories range from mild speculation to absurdity and I am hoping that this book may present a sensible approach to the life of this infamous king.

Egyptologists have been trying to shake off the theory of the curse of Tutankhamun since 1922, to no avail. The so-called curse of the mummy was actually known before the discovery of Tutankhamun but when it was noted that the locals working with

Carter in 1922 believed that entering the tomb activated an ancient curse, he did not deny it, as a means of preventing them entering the tomb at night and disturbing the excavations. Odd events have been reported ever since, starting on the day the entrance was discovered, when the death of Howard Carter's pet canary was said to be caused by a cobra, the symbol of ancient Egyptian royal protection.[2] The curse was also said to have caused an electrical blackout in Cairo at the same time that Lord Carnavon died of an infected insect bite. Egyptian officials could give no suitable explanation for the blackout, although they regularly happen in Cairo, even now, without any rational explanation. In the UK, Lord Carnavon's three-legged dog was recorded as howling at the moment his master died, before dropping down dead. At the time, Carter stated that 'all sane people should dismiss such inventions with contempt'.[3]

Of the thousands of tombs excavated in Egypt, a few do have a 'curse' to deter tomb robbers but Tutankhamun's was not one of them. In 2002, a scientific study was carried out by an Australian scientist, Mark Nelson, to prove or disprove this theory. He looked at the length of time after exposure to the tomb that death occurred. Twenty-five people were potentially susceptible to the curse: those present at the opening of the third door (17th February 1923), the opening of the coffins (3rd February 1926) and the unwrapping of the mummy (11 November 1926). Some people involved in the excavation died at the time, fuelling the curse theories; many lived much longer. Howard Carter died sixteen years later in 1939, aged sixty-five; many visitors, dignitaries and staff working on the tomb survived for over twenty years and others for more than forty, further disproving the curse.[4] The mean age of death for those working on the tomb was seventy years old and the average length of time between death and exposure was thirteen to fifteen years, indicating there is no proof of a curse causing the death of those present in the tomb of Tutankhamun.[5]

Many people view Tutankhamun as a romantic figure, possessing the ability to curse beyond the grave, living in a world of political turmoil and religious zealousness, with a smattering of murder, incest and intrigue thrown in for good measure. Life is rarely like that; as an Egyptologist, I believe it is important to look for the truth, even if at first glance it may not seem as glamorous, romantic or intriguing. Tutankhamun's life was full and rich and this is what will be brought to life in the following pages. Why turn to legends of curses, romanticism and intrigue when the evidence is available to construct an accurate representation of royal life in the late eighteenth dynasty? Life which, to all intents and purposes, is genuinely full of these things.

Numerous ideas and speculations have arisen from the discovery of Tutankhamun and his tomb. There have been almost constant exhibitions, films and novels since 1922: the first exhibition, in 1924, took place before the excavation was even completed. The British Empire Exhibition at Wembley, London, had many pavilions housing exhibitions of the dominions and colonies of the British Empire and an Amusement Park which, amongst other attractions, featured the *Tomb of Tutankhamun*; a reconstruction of the tomb and the finds. The replica artefacts from the exhibition have since been donated to the City of Hull Museum. Between 1961 and 1981, the first major exhibition since the excavation of the artefacts from the tomb, entitled *Treasures of Tutankhamun* travelled the world and brought the treasures to millions of people. Despite expert supervision and care, some exhibits unfortunately suffered from travelling, forcing the Egyptian government to declare the treasures of Tutankhamun would not leave Egypt again.[6] However, in 2005, after many years of deliberation, it was decided that some of the objects were stable enough to travel again. In response to the first exhibition and the initial decision not to allow the objects to leave Egypt, a reconstruction of the tomb was created at the *Tutankhamun Exhibition* in Dorset, UK, which has many beautiful reconstructions of the most famous pieces from his tomb.

Bearing in mind the interest that the public has in Tutankhamun, I am surprised more work has not been done to attempt to re-create the *life* of Tutankhamun as something separate from, albeit just as interesting as, the whole Amarna period. Egyptologists may be put off by the ambiguity of the evidence, which leaves much to assumption and inference and feel safer describing the gold objects from the tomb, which leaves little room for interpretation. I hope to overcome these fears with this book and will make assumptions and inferences from the evidence that is available. I am, of course, aware that alternative views and scenarios may be derived from the available evidence. The main objective of the book is to generate thought and debate about this period. I will take a very different approach to the tomb artefacts, as many were made for the tomb and therefore did not feature in Tutankhamun's life; he may not have even seen many of these items. Through the use of the everyday objects which *were* part of his life, I will introduce the young boy who would be king, as prince and sovereign. These everyday objects may not be covered in gold but they were once held in the hands of the infamous Tutankhamun and are instrumental in piecing together the tapestry of his life.

Archaeological science has advanced since Carter's time. Computerised Tomography (CT scans) of the mummy carried out in 2005 have further added to the story of Tutankhamun. The scans were carried out primarily to prove or disprove the murder theories which have dominated publications on Tutankhamun but the findings also gave much more information which can be tied in with the objects from the tomb, to further elucidate who Tutankhamun was. After the 2005 CT scan had been completed, three international teams reconstructed the face of the boy king, based on the images from the scan. The French and Egyptian teams were told they were reconstructing Tutankhamun's face whereas the American team was not.[7] As would be expected, the basic shape of the reconstructed faces was similar, as they were all based on the same bone structure but, as with all facial reconstructions, the ears, nose and chin were conjectured. Although the nose and chin were different in each reconstruction, the western teams produced similar results. Although this line of study is interesting, it can give little information regarding the individual, as there is a large amount of conjecture about facial features which can completely change its appearance. For example, none of the teams reproduced his rather obvious overbite in their reconstruction, although the top lip does protrude slightly in profile; this however would have been a prominent facial characteristic to the young king's friends. As further technologies become available, information on Tutankhamun's life and family will become clearer.

There is much more evidence available about Tutankhamun than is widely published. Some of this has been available for fifty or sixty years; although it has not often been used in recreating Tutankhamun's reign, it will be here. This evidence comes from his hunting lodges, palaces, mortuary temple and the temples dedicated to a deified form of himself, including the powers with which he was credited by his subjects. There is much more evidence available about Tutankhamun than his tomb and this will be used here, often for the first time, to re-create details of the life of the king.

This book will investigate the personal and political life of Tutankhamun before and after his ascent to the throne, including foreign relations and battles. Although clues to his life are to be found in the tomb, they are not not glamorous or eye-catching; not to found in the golden funerary mask, the coffins or the elaborate jewellery and therefore have often been overlooked. Tutankhamun, the individual, can be found in the board games which he played with his wife, in the clothes and personal items he wore and in the childhood toys adored and treasured by him. Questions will be raised, and answered, such as why Tutankhamun had a number of items belonging to various long-dead family members. Although many Egyptologists focus on his relationship with these family members, my approach is to investigate the emotions behind the treasuring of these heirlooms. Does it really matter if Queen Tiye was his mother, grandmother, or no relation at all? Although it is interesting, surely what is important is that the young boy kept her belongings and even a lock of her hair because she was very dear to him. He missed her when she died and did not want to discard his memories. By the end of the last chapter I hope to have revealed the world of Tutankhamun, hopefully as he saw it, reflecting his views and emotions, which are often lost amidst the glamour of the gold and jewels. Read on and learn about the eighteen rich and full years of Tutankhamun's life.

Some conventions used throughout the book regarding dates and names need to be clarified. Dating any period in ancient Egypt is difficult; the Amarna period especially so. The chronology of ancient Egypt is based on the regnal years of a king, which are then placed into a wider chronology. To know how long a king ruled is not absolute; it relies on what texts are found and the highest regnal date recorded. In the Amarna period, Akhenaten's highest known date is year seventeen, Smenkhkare's is one and Tutankhamun's is nine. Just because higher dates have not been discovered does not mean they did not rule for longer. Therefore, I use the regnal years with an approximate chronological date in brackets; for example, *year 10 (1340 BCE)*, as the regnal years are the only dates we know to be accurate for certain events. The chronological dates vary from publication to publication and cannot be viewed as anything other than an approximation.

Other conventions are in regard to the use of names. At birth, Akhenaten was known as Amenhotep IV; he changed his name in year five (1345 BCE) to show his increasing devotion to the Aten, the sun-disc. The name Akhenaten will be used throughout the book, as this is how he is commonly known. At birth, Tutankhamun was known as Tutankhaten; he changed his name to Tutankhamun after his coronation, to show his devotion to the newly reinstated cult of Amun. As he is best known as Tutankhamun he will be referred to as such throughout the book. The city of Tell el Amarna, adopted by Akhenaten as the new capital for the worship of the sun god, was originally called Akhetaten, 'the horizon of the sun-disc' and throughout the text it will be referred to by this ancient name.

CHAPTER 1

Setting the scene

To fully understand Tutankhamun's life, it is essential to investigate the political and economical background into which he was born, although this is not to be the focus of the entire book. He was the youngest king who ruled in the 'Amarna period' – the period from the rule of the heretic king, Akhenaten (1350 BCE) to the death of King Ay (1320 BCE).

The changes that started the Amarna period began before Akhenaten's reign, during the very traditional reign of his father, Amenhotep III. This period of Egyptian history was seen as a golden age and is a good period to guage the traditions of New Kingdom Egypt and the family background of the young Tutankhamun. Amenhotep III (1386–1349 BCE) was the tenth king of the eighteenth dynasty, the first dynasty of the New Kingdom. He was the son of Thutmosis IV and his secondary wife Mutemwia. Some believe Mutemwia was of foreign origin; the daughter of the Mitannian king, Artatama, sent to Egypt as part of a diplomatic arrangement between Syria and Egypt. The divine birth scene at Luxor temple shows the god Amun impregnating Amenhotep III's mother, the ram-headed god Khnum moulding the new-born king and his *ka* (spirit) on a potter's wheel and Hathor and Mut helping Mutemwia nurse her new-born son; so showing his divinity and that, from the start, he was a traditional king dedicated to a number of gods.

Amenhotep III and his chief royal wife, Tiye, had at least six children; two sons and four daughters. Queen Tiye was of noble but not royal birth; in marrying her, Amenhotep III flouted convention, as traditionally kings married royal princesses. Tiye was regularly shown alongside her husband in a complimentary, rather than inferior position and was often represented in her own right without the king. Akhenaten was their youngest son, named Amenhotep at birth; only later did he change his name. The young sons of Amenhotep III were brought up in the palace of Memphis, where they were trained in the athletic arts: hunting lions, wild ass and gazelles, charioteering and archery. Amenhotep III was often shown participating in sports of this kind; indeed, his great-grandfather Thutmosis III was a great warrior king and the first empire builder in Egypt. It was natural for Amenhotep III to want his sons to share his skills. In reliefs of his later years, Akhenaten is rarely shown performing these traditional acts of kingly prowess, which some suggest indicates a lack of interest or skill.

Because the young princes were brought up in Memphis, they were exposed to a prominent solar cult. Near Memphis lay Heliopolis, the site of the most creation myth, where the primeval mound rose from the primeval waters, giving birth to the first dawn. At Heliopolis, the solar deities Atum, Re, Khepri and Horakhty were worshipped and the young princes would have known their rituals and the cult. Since the Middle Kingdom, the power and popularity of the solar cult had risen; it was so popular that most local deities 'solarised' their names by adding 'Re', including Amun, who became Amun-Re. The new solar age also saw the introduction of new funerary texts, including the *Book of What is in the Amduat* and the *Litany of Re*, which introduced the 'Aten' (in reference to the sun disc), which later dominated the Amarna period and Tutankhamun's early years. Although the

Aten is associated primarily with the reign of Akhenaten, during the reign of Amenhotep III it was, more than any other deity, increasingly mentioned in connection with the royal barque, the palace and some royal names; indicating that during Akhenaten's childhood and early adulthood the solar cult was incredibly prominent, with the sun as the Aten, or sun disc, increasing in importance.

Despite this increase in the power and influence of the Aten, the cult of Amun-Ra, a solar creator god, was dominant, especially in the Theban region, the religious capital of the New Kingdom. The temple at Karnak, dedicated to this deity, was the wealthiest in Egypt and its priesthood the most powerful. Throughout the eighteenth dynasty, its power and wealth had started to rival the king's, which is often believed to be the cause of Akhenaten's religious revolution; a means to limit the growing power of the priests. The power of the priesthood of Amun had increased so much they were able to play an active role in the choice of heir to the throne. Amenhotep III's father, Thutmosis IV, removed this privilege, proclaiming himself, at the command of the solar god of the sphinx at Giza, Horemkhu-Kheper-Ra-Atum, heir.[1] The slow rise of the cult of the Aten during the reign of Amenhotep III further limited the power of the Amun priesthood.

Amenhotep's main achievement in his thirty-eight-year reign was in foreign policy. Through a number of diplomatic marriages, in the tradition of his father and great-grandfather Thutmosis III, Amenhotep III cemented a number of political alliances. The full extent of political relationships during the reign of Amenhotep III is shown in the 'Amarna Letters', a collection of more than 380 tablets written in cuneiform, the international diplomatic language of the time. The letters were discovered in 1887 by a local Egyptian woman who was digging for fertiliser. Although she destroyed some, she saw there was writing on them and sold the remainder to another villager. The letters are from foreign kings, the rulers of Babylon, Mitanni (Syria) and Arzawa (south-western Anatolia), to Amenhotep III and Akhenaten; one may perhaps be to Tutankhamun. The foreign kings write to the Egyptian king as the superior ruler of an economically strong country, asking for gold, which 'is like the sand in Egypt, you simply gather it up'.[2] In exchange for golden diplomatic gifts, the foreign kings sent their daughters and sisters to marry the Egyptian king, bearing expensive 'wedding gifts'. Amenhotep had two Mitannian, at least one Anatolian and two Babylonian wives (although there may have been more; his harem is thought to have contained over 1000 women).

It is clear from the letters that Egypt was the superior nation. The Babylonian king, Kadashman-Edil I, tried to test the boundaries of the relationship by requesting an Egyptian bride. He was told, in no uncertain terms, that Egyptian brides were never sent abroad. Kadashman-Edil also complained that Amenhotep III constantly kept his messengers waiting – one for over six years. As the superior in the relationship, the Egyptian king was within his rights to keep them waiting but Amenhotep III did not hide his mistrust of the Babylonian messengers, believing them to be dishonest and untrustworthy. Some archaeologists believe these letters, coupled with archaeological evidence, show that, from as early as the start of the eighteenth dynasty (about 1570 BCE), Egypt had a number of colony-states in Syria-Palestine. Artefacts indicate that the area was divided into three regions; Amurru, Upe and Canaan, each ruled by a vassal ruler under the power of the Egyptian king.[3]

The economy of Egypt was particularly strong during the reign of Amenhotep III, primarily because of the trade arising from strong international alliances, as well as gold mining in the Wadi Hammamat and Kush.[4] There was no warfare during his reign, meaning that Amenhotep could concentrate on building projects in Egypt. The palace of Malkata was a particularly large effort, although all that is left are the mud brick foundations and painted plaster fragments. His mortuary temple, on the west bank of the Nile at Thebes, was reputed to have been the biggest and most beautiful in Egypt. This has also disappeared; only the two colossi of Amenhotep (now known as the Colossi of Memnon), which originally stood at the pylon gateway remain, standing alone in an otherwise empty field. For many years, due to the damage caused by an earthquake in 27 BCE, they moaned at dawn, causing Greek travellers to give them the name 'Colossi of Memnon', in reference to the mythological Memnon crying for his mother Eos, the goddess of the dawn. Current excavations at the site have uncovered fragmentary remains and further statues within the temple. Amenhotep also built and decorated a large part of the temple at Luxor, which was completed by Tutankhamun, as well as the third pylon and the complex of Mut at Karnak. Mut stands just outside the current enclosure walls and includes an unusual horseshoe-shaped sacred lake and a sanctuary filled with more than seven hundred life-size statues of the goddess Sekhmet, the goddess of epidemics. The statues are thought to have been commissioned near the end of his reign, when Amenhotep was suffering from unspecified illness.

Between years 16 and 27 of Amenhotep III's reign (1370–1359 BCE), his oldest son and heir, Thutmosis, died, leaving his youngest son, Akhenaten, as heir to the throne. Akhenaten is often described as a sickly youth, although there is no real information about his health; this assumption is primarily based on the epithet he chose to use in later life, 'Great in his Duration' (meaning 'long-lived'), which may have been an expression of hope, in the expectation of leading a short life. Although Akhenaten only reigned for seventeen years in the eighteenth dynasty (1350–33 BCE) he is one of the most written-about kings of ancient Egypt. He is the subject of many bizarre and interesting theories which often have little, outdated or no evidence to support them. One thing

that is certain is that Akhenaten single-handedly changed the
religion of Egypt from the worship of a pantheon to the worship
of one god.

During the early years of his reign, Akhenaten slowly elevated
the Aten, or sun disc, to the principal god; totally eliminating all
other gods by year nine (1341 BCE). However, the Aten was only
worshipped by the royal family; everyone else was expected to
worship Akhenaten, who was named the 'only son of Aten'. This
angered many people: the priests, who made their living from the
gods, the officials, who may have invested in the temple, and the
ordinary people whose personal religion was now dictated for
them. This anger encouraged the revilement of Akhenaten, carried
out after his reign by Tutankhamun, Ay and Horemheb.

The only way to the Aten was through the worship of
Akhenaten. He truly believed he was equal to the god and is shown
performing rituals and festivals alongside him, as if they were performing them together. The most important of these festivals was
the *heb sed* (rejuvenation festival), which was performed every
thirty years to demonstrate the king was still physically fit and able
to rule. The king had to run around six markers, which represented
the length and breadth of Egypt. If he was successful, he kept his
kingship. The Aten was the only god who celebrated a *heb sed* and
these correspond with those of Akhenaten.

Akhenaten also enclosed the name of the Aten into a cartouche,
in the manner of a king; it is the first and only time this had ever
been done. He could have been raising the divinity of kingship to
the higher level of a complete god, or lowering the status of the god
to match that of the king. Either way, he considered himself equal
to the god and therefore worthy of worship. Even the throne name
adopted by Nefertiti hints at the new elevation of her husband,
Akhenaten, to the status of a god. Traditionally, titles adopted as
throne names were of the types 'Mery-Ra' (Beloved of Ra), or
'Mery-Ptah' (Beloved of Ptah). However Nefertiti's throne name,

'Mery-Waenra', means 'Beloved of Waenra' (the throne name of Akhenaten), suggesting that, uniquely to his reign, he had replaced the traditional gods used for this type of title or epithet.[5]

Despite the remarkable changes instigated by Akhenaten, it is often stated that for many years (some believe as many as twelve) of his seventeen-year reign he co-ruled with his father, Amenhotep III. Various pieces of evidence support this, but there are many gaps – enough to leave some doubt – and a number of Egyptologists do not believe this co-regency took place. If there was a co-regency between Amenhotep III and Akhenaten, it is thought that Amenhotep III ruled from Thebes and his wife Tiye lived in Akhetaten with her son Akhenaten. However, a household shrine in Akhetaten shows a stela of an ageing Amenhotep III alongside his queen. This could suggest that while Tiye was in Akhetaten, her husband was still alive and visited or perhaps even briefly lived in the city.

The third pylon at Karnak, built by Amenhotep III, shows him presenting Akhenaten to Amun and could illustrate the time that the co-regency was announced. The inscription under the image of Akhenaten states: 'I rule by his agreement, I join with his strength, I take possession of his power'.[6] In any decision regarding ascent to the throne, whether as king or co-regent, it was traditional for the oracle of Amun to be addressed, to gain the god's support. The oracle of Amun was very prominent during the New Kingdom and he could be approached about various issues, by royalty and non-royals, although non-royal people would have used a priest as an intermediary or ask the god in procession, as it was not possible for them to enter the temples. Amun was often approached to legitimise the heir to the throne, by showing his divine approval and the pylon scene represents this support. The co-regency theory has a number of consequences for the time line of this turbulent period and even affects the arguments regarding the parentage of Tutankhamun, which will be discussed in Chapter 3.

Although there is doubt about the co-regency, there is no doubt that Queen Tiye held a prominent position in Akhetaten. She is often depicted being revered by Akhenaten and his wife Nefertiti and participating in public duties. Records show she even helped with foreign affairs: a number of the international Amarna letters, discovered in the so-called 'foreign office' at Akhetaten, are addressed to her.[7] Amenhotep III may have asked her to accompany Akhenaten to his new city, to ensure that, at least in the early years, he did not make any drastic decisions or changes that could cause unrest or economic and political harm. Perhaps he was aware of the instability of his son's mental health and wanted to provide him with a 'voice of reason'. Tiye is often presented as dominating her son and it is suggested she was behind many of the religious changes. However, there is no irrefutable evidence for this.

It is clear that Akhenaten was close to his mother; this seems to be common throughout the Amarna period. Queen Tiye is represented in many family scenes with Akhenaten, Nefertiti and their daughters. If these are to be believed, she featured highly in the day-to-day life of her son, although Monsterrat suggests that this show of family solidarity may have been a propaganda tool; a united front against the rest of the population who possibly opposed the religious changes.[8] The only family member missing from these scenes is Amenhotep III, who ruled from Thebes and was not part of the Amarna revolution. Whether or not the images of a united family were propaganda, it is clear that Akhenaten trusted Tiye to help him with administration.

In year 30 (1346 BCE), when Tiye moved to Akhetaten, her daughter Sitamun married her father Amenhotep III and was raised to the status of 'Great Royal Wife' in the Theban region, in her mother's place. It was considered normal for kings to marry their daughters or granddaughters, to ensure they were unable to marry outside the royal family and thus, potentially, weaken the power of the throne. Some of these marriages were purely political and there were no children; others did produce offspring. In the case of Sitamun and her father, whether this marriage was purely political is questionable. Sitamun replaced her mother Tiye as 'Great Royal Wife' (the equivalent of 'First Lady') and accompanied the king in religious rituals and at state events.

By the time Tiye moved to Akhetaten with her son, Akhenaten had already instigated a number of changes, showing his growing devotion to the god Aten. It is possible that this increased favour may have been a subtle retaliation to and curbing of the extreme power of the cult of Amun, in the temple of Karnak. He may have been following his grandfather, Thutmosis IV's, lead in slowly removing the power of the priesthood. Within the first four years of his reign (1350–46 BCE), Akhenaten began to search for a suitable site to erect a new temple to his god. He wanted a site that had never been used for the worship of other gods. He started his search in the deserts surrounding the Nile Valley, then apparently went south, to Nubia. He had originally been sent there, to the temples of Soleb and Sedeinga, by his father to oversee the carving of the *heb sed* reliefs celebrating the festival of Amenhotep III in year 30 (1346 BCE). Akhenaten was probably responsible for organising the celebrations, which lasted for anything up to eight months; perhaps his father's way of keeping his young co-ruler busy. While Akhenaten was in Nubia preparing the celebrations, in Thebes further celebrations were planned and new monuments constructed to commemorate the festival. The colossi of Memnon, which stood before the mortuary temple of Amenhotep III at Thebes were erected and now, apart from a few fragments, are all that remain of this enormous temple.[9]

Akhenaten constructed a village between the second and third cataracts of the Nile, near the modern town of Sese in the district of Sudla (modern Sesebi) in the Sudan. Excavations show a small town within a large boundary wall, which can be dated to the reign of Akhenaten through the discovery of his foundation deposits.[10] (Foundation deposits were buried at the start of any building project, to identify the builder and consisted of objects such as seals, pottery and model tools.) The town consisted of two temples and what is likely to have been a royal residence. It was structured in an orderly manner, with very straight roads and compact streets and is comparable to the ground plan of the later city of Akhetaten. It was clearly built as a single project, with no sign of natural growth. Each house was built flush against that of its neighbour, without any land or gardens; they may have been built only to house the king and his court during the Amenhotep III *heb sed*, although the site was in use until the Ramesside period.[11] Most of the houses had a large outer room with four smaller rooms leading from it. There were a few larger houses belonging to the overseers and officials. These had an anteroom leading from the entrance that led to a hall and central living room, with smaller rooms off it. There was also a door that led to the owner's private apartment; bathroom, dressing room and bedroom. These houses, like most in Egypt, were probably used for business as well as for living.

Both temples at this settlement had a large courtyard at the front and follow a traditional temple design, which included inner and outer hypostyle halls, a sanctuary and some subsidiary chambers.[12] The site does not seem to have been completed by Akhenaten, who left shortly after the *heb sed* celebrations were complete. In one of the temples, north of the hypostyle hall, a shaft was cut into the floor leading to a crypt with images of Akhenaten and Nefertiti in a slightly distorted form, typical of the art of the early years of his reign. They are shown worshipping a number of deities including Shu, Geb, Atum, Osiris and Maat-Re (Lord of Nubia,), proving that the abandonment of the gods had not then begun.

The temples were dedicated to the Theban triad, Amun, Mut and Khonsu and the worship was traditional, with the statue of the god housed within a darkened sanctuary at the rear of the temple, to which the priests made offerings twice daily.[13] Akhenaten also built a small solar temple just outside the central sacred precinct, which may be an indication of his growing adoration of the solar god. It is here that the Aten's name is first attested during this reign.[14] However, the Aten is named alongside other solar deities, indicating that at this stage he was part of the wider solar cycle and not a god independent of the solar pantheon. He was depicted as a falcon-headed human, similar in appearance to the much older deity, Re-Horakhty.

In these early years, Akhenaten also travelled to Kawa in Nubia, where there was a temple built by his father and dedicated to Amun. Akhenaten built an Aten temple at the site; the small settlement there was called 'Gem-Aten' (the Aten is found). This town was inhabited from this period; and remains at the site date to the sixth century BCE. During his reign, Tutankhamun added to the temple of Amenhotep III at Kawa.

It is possible that before building the city at Tell el Amarna Akhenaten wanted to make the Aten's presence and his rising importance known; the easiest way was to build Aten temples alongside those of Amun at Karnak. Akhenaten built a large temple dedicated to Aten within the boundaries of the temple of Amun at Karnak and constructed it in a fashion unlike anything the Egyptians had ever seen – perhaps an indication of his early shunning of tradition.

The temple was constructed using *talatat* blocks, an innovation of his reign. *Talatat* were small blocks, one hand high by one hand deep and one hand wide, which enabled quick building, as each block could be handled by one individual. The basic temple structure was traditional, with some ten pylons decorated with colossal images of Akhenaten and Nefertiti making offerings to the gods.[15] There were also a number of pillared halls containing colossal statues of Akhenaten in rather bizarre form; these presently adorn the Louvre, Luxor Museum and Cairo Museum. These are elongated forms of the king, with rounded hips and thighs and in some examples, naked, but without genitalia; perhaps to show his androgynous nature, in the same manner as his new god, the Aten. The rituals carried out in this temple were different from the other temples and shrines at the site. Rather than focusing on the darkened sanctuary at the rear of the temple where the statue of the god was housed, the temple rituals focused on offering tables; the foundations of over three thousand tables have been discovered at this site.[16] The offering tables were piled high with food to spiritually nourish the Aten. Many are inscribed with the name of Nefertiti, giving her a prominent role in the temple worship of the Aten, something not seen for any other queen. The unusual worshipping practices and prominence of the queen at this new temple should have made it clear, if not to the people of Thebes, then at least to the priesthood of Amun at Karnak, that there were changes ahead. Recovered *talatat* blocks indicate that he may also have built a palace there for ceremonial purposes. This palace is thought to have included a Window of Appearances – a key feature of Amarna royal policy – through which the king and queen favoured their courtiers with gifts of gold jewellery.[17]

After these temples were complete and his dedication to the new cult had progressed, Akhenaten was unhappy with the Aten sharing space with other gods and continued his search for a site where he could build his new solar city. Whether the Nubian town of Sesi was seriously contemplated by Akhenaten for his new solar city or whether its consideration was simply a means of demonstrating Egyptian dominance in Nubia (traditional foreign policy in the New Kingdom) is uncertain, but it was not long before he travelled north and set up his town at the modern site of Tell el Amarna. The Nubian site may not have been suitable for a solar cult, due to the abnormally high levels of rainfall, attested by a drainage system excavated by the gates within the enclosure wall.[18] Amarna was preferable, situated in a region with low annual rainfall. It has been suggested that the Nubian site may also have been too remote and, not being within the boundaries of Egypt, an unsuitable city for promoting the young king and the new religion.[19] If Nubia had been chosen as the site of the new religion, how different might the Amarna period have been? Would the cult have developed in the same way? Would it have affected Egypt to such an extent if the city had been outside Egyptian borders? These are speculations; the new city dedicated to the Aten was built at Akhetaten (modern Tell el Amarna) in middle Egypt. From year nine (1341 BCE), it was the capital city of Egypt, the focus of Akhenaten's new religion, and possibly the birthplace and childhood home of Tutankhamun.

CHAPTER 2

Akhetaten: a new beginning

In year nine (1341 BCE) of Akhenaten's reign, the entire royal court moved from the religious capital of Thebes to Akhetaten, 250 miles north of Thebes and 200 miles south of Memphis. Thebes had been the religious capital since the start of the New Kingdom (about 1570 BCE) and had maintained its status for more than two hundred years, focused primarily on Karnak and the cult of Amun. To quash the power of the Amun cult, Akhenaten wanted to build a city entirely dedicated to his new god, the Aten, whose power rose quickly in the first four years of his reign. He chose Akhetaten and it was possibly here that Tutankhamun was born.

Akhenaten chose the site at Tell el Amarna after divine intervention, believing the Aten had led him there. Modern Egyptologists suggest this 'intervention' may have been a dip in the eastern cliffs that resembled the hieroglyphic sign for horizon and which Akhenaten may have taken as a sign that this site was overlooked by the god Aten. On certain days of the year the sun would rise in this dip, further mirroring the hieroglyphic sign. The location of this city, between Memphis (the administrative capital) and Thebes (the religious capital), was planned so the new city could take on the roles of both these important cities. Studies by Michael Mallinson (of the Egypt Exploration Society of London) have indicated that the two principal temples at Akhetaten were based on architectural elements of the temples of Karnak and Heliopolis, as an attempt to represent both major cities within this one settlement.[1] Despite the increased importance of this site as the capital city, evidence shows that the royal palaces of Memphis (where Akhenaten and his brother were brought up) and Gurob, in the Faiyum, were also used during this period.

On the boundary stelae surrounding the new city, demarcating the boundaries of the site, Akhenaten's divine message is recorded in all its glory:

> Now it is the Aten, my father, who advised me concerning it – namely Akhetaten. No official had ever advised me concerning it, nor had any people in the entire land ever advised me concerning it, to tell me to make Akhetaten in this distant place.[2]

Everything in the new city of Akhetaten was oriented towards the east, including the cemeteries, which were often placed in the west, representing the deceased's journey mirroring that of the setting sun. On one of the boundary stelae, Akhenaten gave directions to be buried 'where the sun rises' – not in the traditional western realm, where the sun sets, something he believed was too closely tied up with the traditional religion and had no place in his new cult of the Aten.

By year four (1346 BCE) of Akhenaten's reign, work had begun on defining the boundaries of this new city of Akhetaten, and in year five (1345 BCE) three stelae were set up identifying the boundaries and describing how Akhenaten chose the site and dedicated it to the Aten. In year six (1344 BCE), there were fourteen boundary stelae, which show Akhenaten, Nefertiti and two of their daughters (Meritaten and Meketaten) worshipping the Aten, displayed as a sun disc with emanating rays, each ending in a hand resting upon the royal family's heads. Exactly one year from the time the building work began on the city, it was ready to be inhabited. Akhetaten covered a total area of over 200 square kilometres (77 square miles); a large space to plan and irrigate in such a short time. The area was not all settlement but included agricultural land, on the west bank of the Nile, and the cemetery. However the speed with which the city was constructed could suggest it was built with many cut corners and using inferior building techniques. In year five (1345 BCE), it is recorded that Akhenaten rode around the boundary stelae, and therefore the boundaries of the city, in an electrum (an alloy of gold and silver) chariot. Some scholars have misinterpreted his vow to mean he would never step outside of the boundaries of his city again:[3]

> I shall not make Akhetaten for him south of it, north of it, west of it or east of it. I shall not go past the southern stela of Akhetaten towards the south, nor shall I go past the northern stela of Akhetaten downstream, making Akhetaten there. Nor shall I make it for him on the western side of Akhetaten but I shall make Akhetaten for the Aten, my father, on the eastern side of Akhetaten, the place which he himself made to be enclosed for him by the mountain.[4]

This should be interpreted as a vow that the *city* would not extend past these boundaries but would remain within the originally demarcated area.[5]

By year nine (1341 BCE) of Akhenaten, the entire royal court had moved from the traditional religious capital at Thebes to Akhetaten. However, the only officials who moved either served a function within the city or the cult of Aten. The city was predominately inhabited by artists, temple scribes and militia; there was only one vizier and a handful of administrators. It was primarily a religious capital, devoted to the worship of the Aten and serving Akhenaten and his family. This is supported by the archaeological record, which suggests the first buildings to be erected here were the palaces and temples of the Central City area, in the middle of the plain on the eastern side of the Nile. The limited number of administrators could suggest either that Amenhotep III, in Thebes, was in control of the administration of Egypt, leaving religious issues to Akhenaten or that Akhenaten had little concern for politics, economics or administration and concentrated primarily on his interests: the Aten and his own divinity.

Despite the peculiar function of the city, between twenty and fifty thousand people lived at Akhetaten during the height of Akhenaten's reign, ten per cent of whom were elite. Although the city was not fortified, it was closed off to any who did not have a function within it; a strong military presence ensured this was enforced. The location of the city, on the open valley of the El Amarna plain, meant it was easily policed and protected.[6] The estates of the elite also housed their servants either in small houses close to the main house or within the main house in small self-contained suites. However, as the years went by, a poorer class of housing developed to the north of the Amarna plain, indicated by a few small houses lining the ditches used to drain refuse from the rest of the town. The wealth of the homeowners was very much reflected in the size and grandeur of their houses: some of the larger houses had gates big enough for a horse-chariot to pass through easily – an indication of wealth and status.

It is thought the chariot was a general mode of transport in this city, rather than a purely military or hunting vehicle. The king and queen favoured it as a method of transport. They travelled daily down the 'King's Road', the central street in the city (known in Arabic as *Sikketel Sultan*) by chariot, in a procession seen by all their favoured officials who (no doubt) cheered and clapped as they rode by. The procession started at the North Riverside Palace and continued south towards the Great Palace and the King's House, probably stopping at the Great Aten Temple and the Small Aten Temple on the way, to leave offerings for the god.

The city was planned around the official centres of palaces, temples and military barracks. Shops, taverns or schools, as we think of them, do not appear to have existed, although it is unlikely that a large city could survive without them. The lack of buildings with these specific functions suggests that these activities either took place in the open or in non-specialised buildings. Children may have been educated in the houses of scribes, or in public areas, leaving little evidence, and the market place was anywhere someone wanted to trade, with no need for an official structure. However, factories and workshops do seem to have been run within the houses – workshops discovered at Akhetaten were closely associated with private houses. Within these houses, there was an area reserved for the workshop and separated from the living quarters, enabling the workmen to work from home. These workshops included centres of glass and faience production, for which Amarna was particularly famous; a number of 'factories' continued producing faience until halfway through the reign of Tutankhamun. The home and adjoining workshop of the sculptor Thutmose, in the sculptors' quarter, is one of the most famous; it has produced a large number of stone sculptures in various stages of completion, left behind when the city was abandoned at the end of Akhenaten's reign and following the subsequent collapse of the Aten cult.

Statues and votive objects of the traditional gods have also been discovered in Thutmose's workshop, indicating that the people of Akhetaten did not totally abandon the traditional religion, despite the show of devotion to Akhenaten they were no doubt displaying. Various amulets and votive objects of the traditional gods have also been found in many of the houses at Akhetaten, including the house of the High Priest of the Aten, which is most surprising. These votive objects include amulets of Bes, Hathor, Isis and the Eye of Horus. They may have been produced at the site (in workshops such as Thutmose's) or could have been imported from other cities in Egypt. This indicates that the new religion was not strongly enforced by Akhenaten.[7] However, he was very isolated in his self-created world and did not venture into the homes of his officials. As long as they *appeared* to adhere solely to his religion, he was satisfied.

Ordinary people were not allowed to enter either traditional temples or the new Aten temples, which were only open to the royal family and the priests. They worshipped in their homes. Even before the religious revolution, solar gods were rarely worshipped in the home; the new god, Aten, did not seem to offer anything that the people felt they could bring into their houses. The domestic religion was more difficult to control than the state religion; although Akhenaten closed the traditional temples and diverted the revenue to Akhetaten it was impossible to change people's basic beliefs; especially as public worship was not a feature of the religion. Likewise, the funerary beliefs of the general populace of Amarna did not appear to change; excepting those officials with rock-cut tombs, it is thought that many citizens sent their dead 'home' to their villages to be buried traditionally in family tombs outside Akhetaten, thereby ensuring a traditional afterlife. The 2006 excavation at Tell el Amarna uncovered a large cemetery used by the poorer people; it could be the final resting place of those who could not afford to transport their relatives' bodies out of the city. Very little information on these burials was available at the time of writing, as the excavation work was too recent. A traditional after-life meant a rebirth into the 'Field of Reeds' (rather like paradise), ruled by the god Osiris. The funerary beliefs were closely tied in to the solar cycle; people believed that just as the sun sets at dusk and rises again at dawn, so the deceased die (set) and are reborn (rise). According to the religion of the Aten, at sunset the world dies and can only live again once the sun has risen at dawn. There was no nocturnal journey for the Aten, in the same manner as the other solar gods. Taking away the day-to-day religion of the people was bad enough but when Akhenaten took away their hope of a peaceful and prosperous eternity after death, it was too much to take and difficult to implement.

Excavations of the workshop of Thutmose produced numerous images of the royal family in various stages of completion. The most famous is the painted bust of Nefertiti (presently in Berlin), showing that Thutmose was not merely a sculptor, but a *royal* sculptor, and may have been lucky enough to have the queen sit for him during its making. This bust has caused many discussions over the years, as it shows Nefertiti with only one eye. Some have questioned why she is depicted in this manner and whether it shows she had a disease resulting in the loss of an eye or cataracts. The simple fact, often overlooked in these discussions, is that this bust was unfinished and, as it was found in a workshop, was probably never used. The eye has been examined many times: there appear to be small traces of glue, indicating that an eye *was* inlaid in the socket but subsequently fell out. This image is often taken to be a true portrait of Nefertiti, although there is no identifying inscription; all that identifies it as her is the distinctive headdress that only she is ever shown wearing. As beautiful as the bust is to the modern mind, it is possible (although there is no evidence to prove it) that Nefertiti herself did not like it, hence it was still in the workshop, incomplete and unused. Or perhaps she died before the bust could be used, rendering it surplus to requirements. Whatever the answer, the place it was found has to be an important factor in the interpretation. There were also a number of unfinished heads of Akhenaten, and more than twenty portraits of the royal family and elite non-royal individuals. These heads were carved for use on statues and would have been attached to a body of the same stone; the join covered with a necklace or wig. The heads of the villagers are thought to be actual portraits, perhaps personally commissioned for their funerary chapels, whereas the royal faces are thought to be stylised images, due to their similarity in structure.

For example, three quartzite heads of the Amarna princesses, the half-sisters of Tutankhamun, all have shaved, elongated, skulls. Rather than accepting them as stylised, albeit a unique stylisation, scholars have discussed what ailments these heads could depict. The most commonly accepted theory is that the princesses may have suffered from hydrocephalus (water on the brain). Other ideas include artificial head deformation, which, although it would produce an elongated head, is not known to be practiced in ancient Egypt. It is more likely that these heads were symbolic, although of what exactly is not clear. If viewed from the rear, the shape of the heads resembles an egg, which some have suggested connects with the cosmic egg of creation, from which all life emanated. This would therefore represent the divinity of the princesses as daughters of the 'son of Aten', Akhenaten.

Akhetaten also included a workmen's village, similar to Deir el Medina in the Theban region, which was built for the workmen of the Valley of the Kings. As Deir el Medina was closed during this period, many of the workmen probably transferred directly to Akhetaten to construct the royal cemetery there. The workmen's village at Akhetaten was similar in size to Deir el Medina, with approximately seventy to eighty houses surrounded by an enclosure wall. The village was relatively self-sufficient; cottage gardens provided vegetables and livestock were kept, although water had to be brought from outside, either from the Nile (two miles away) or from communal wells. Excavations have shown that pigs were kept in the village, which is unusual, as these animals were considered unclean and the ancient Egyptians did not eat them. However pigs clearly had an economic use – the villagers probably used them to eat waste food.

Like the rest of the city, the village paid only lip service to the new religion. Excavation of many of the houses has uncovered amulets of Bes, Taweret and Hathor and murals of Bes painted on some of the walls show that household religion remained loyal to tradition. The continued worship of the traditional domestic gods indicates the religion of Akhenaten was not as successful as he believed, which led to a quick and easy transition from the new religion back to the old. The main problem with the new religion of the Aten was that it was closely tied in with the cult of the king and offered very little to the ordinary worker. This would not encourage them to give up their traditional gods, who could be approached on various aspects of life: fertility, health, sexual pleasure and justice.

As would be expected in such a religious city, there were numerous temples at Akhetaten, all dedicated to the Aten and only entered by the priests and the royal family, which may have included the young prince Tutankhamun. These temples were different in style and function to traditional Egyptian temples, as the nature of the principal god had changed. A traditional temple was dark and enclosed, with the first pillared courtyard, behind the pylon gateway, often being the only part open to the sky. As the visitor progressed through the temple the floors got higher and the ceilings lower until the sanctuary, a small dark room, was reached. This housed the statue of the god, kept locked within a small shrine. The temples of the Aten at Akhetaten were open-roofed, not shadowy and dark. There was no need for a cult statue; in an open-roofed temple the object of worship, the sun, was always visible. The processional way, which normally ended in a dark sanctuary, here ended at an elevated altar, upon which offerings were left to be touched by the rays of the sun. Beneath the open roof the king and priests were able to witness the god in every corner of the temple. There were dedicatory stelae and many offering tables, constantly covered with traditional offerings of bread, beer, fowl, oxen and geese. The temple had its own slaughterhouse so that ritual sacrifices could be carried out nearby. The rays of the sun touched the offerings, absorbing spiritual nourishment from them; they were then distributed to the priests of the Aten.

Shaded temples were also built at Akhetaten, purely for the royal women, enabling them to worship in their own accommodation.

These were built to the south of the Amarna plain and allowed the royal ladies to escape the hustle and bustle of the city. These temples were built on a north-south axis, to catch the north wind and were constructed of kiosk sanctuaries, with screen walls to allow draughts of air to circulate.[8] The temples were elaborately decorated and were pleasant places for the royal ladies to spend their time. Although the temples were open-roofed the temple structure was similar to a traditional temple, with pylons, courtyards and columned halls. Surviving images of the main temple of the Aten from Akhetaten show the pylon was adorned with ten flagpoles, two more than Karnak. In the colonnaded halls were colossal statues of the king and queen, the only statues housed in the temple, indicating that they were a focus of veneration in the daily temple worship.

Worshipping was different at Akhetaten; the Aten did not speak, so there was no 'Holy Book' or mythology surrounding him, whereas all other deities were part of a rich mythological history. The Aten was presented as a disc, with emanating rays ending in hands holding *ankh*, or symbols of life (although these were only ever given to the royal family). This imagery represents the light radiating from the solar disc and was merely one element of the iconography of the wider solar cult.

Akhenaten believed he received all his information and teachings directly from the Aten, though not as a prophet but rather as an element of the god himself. He then placed a 'Teaching' or 'Instruction' into the heart of his subjects, probably orally; there is no surviving written evidence of these teachings. Possibly, through the 'Window of Appearances', Akhenaten himself may have lectured the chosen on matters of the Aten, although for the greater populus of Akhetaten, the Priests of the Aten no doubt led the instructions. The 'Great Hymn to the Aten' recorded in the tomb of Ay at Amarna is believed to have been written by Akhenaten. If so, perhaps he would have taught it to his wives, including Nefertiti and Kiya and his children. Tutankhamun may have learned the hymn at his mother's knee:

Splendid you rise in heaven's lightland, O living Aten, the creator of life! When you have dawned in eastern lightland you have filled every land with your beauty. You are beauteous, great, radiant, high over every land; your rays embrace the lands to the limit of all that you have made: being Re, you reach the limits. You bend them for your beloved son. Though you are far away, your rays are on earth, though one sees you, your strides are unseen.

When you set in the western lightland, the land is in darkness, in the manner of death. One sleeps in chambers, head covered, one eye does not see the other. Were they robbed of their goods that are under their heads? People would not remark it. Every lion comes from his den; all serpents, they bite. Darkness hovers and the earth is silent. As their maker rests in lightland.

Earth brightens when you dawn in the lightland, when you shine as the Aten of daytime. As you dispel the dark, as you cast your rays. The Two Lands (*Egypt*) are in festivity. Awake they stand upon their feet, you have roused them; bodies cleansed, clothed, their arms adore your appearance. The entire land sets out to work. All beasts browse on their herbs; trees, herbs are sprouting, birds fly from their nests, their wings greeting your *ka* (spirit). All flocks frisk on their feet, all that fly up and alight, they live when you dawn for them. Ships fare north, fare south as well, roads lie open when you rise; the fish in the river dart before you; your rays are in the midst of the sea.

Who makes seed grow in women, who creates people from sperm; who feeds the son in his mother's womb, who soothes him to still his tears. You nurse [even] in the womb, who gives breath to nourish all that he has made. When he comes from the womb to breathe, on the day when he is born, you open wide his mouth. You supply his needs. When the chick in the egg speaks within the shell, you give him breath within it to sustain him. When you have made him complete, to break out from the egg, he comes out from the egg, to announce his completion, walking on his legs he comes from it.

How many are your deeds, though hidden from sight. O sole god, beside whom there is none! You made the world as you wished, you alone. All people, herds and flocks; all upon earth that walk on legs, all on high that fly on wings. The lands of Khor and Kush, the land of Egypt, you set every man in his place, you supply their needs. Everyone has his food and his lifetime is counted. Their tongues differ in speech and their characters likewise; their skins are distinct, for you distinguished the peoples.

You made a Nile in the underworld, you bring him when you will, to nourish the people [of Egypt], for you made them for yourself. The Lord of all who toils for them, Lord of all Lands who shines for them. Aten of daytime, great in glory! All distant lands, you make them live, you have made a heavenly Nile descend for them, he makes waves on the mountains like the sea, to drench their fields and their towns. How excellent are your plans, O lord of eternity!

A Nile from heaven, for the foreign peoples and all lands' creatures that walk on legs, for Egypt the Nile that comes from the Netherworld.

Your rays nurse all fields. When you shine they live, they grow for you. You made the seasons to foster all that you made. Winter to cool them, heat that they taste you. You made the far sky to shine therein, to behold all that you made. You alone, shining in your form of living Aten, risen, radiant, distant, near. You have made millions of forms from yourself alone, towns, villages, fields, the river's course; all eyes observe you upon them, for you are the Aten of daytime on high.

During the early years of Akhenaten's reign, while he was establishing his new capital, other temples in Egypt were still functioning. Correspondence has survived from year four (1346 BCE), when the High Priest of Amun was sent on a quarrying expedition, presumably to find stone for construction within the temple of Amun. The High Priest of Ptah at Memphis also reported to Akhenaten that all was well at his temple, showing that the worship of Ptah and Amun was still tolerated at this early stage. Akhenaten did not halt the worship of other deities until after year five (1345 BCE) and it was not until year nine (1341 BCE) that persecution of other temples began, especially the cult of Amun, against which he took particular umbrage. His men erased the name of Amun from all monuments, scarabs and obelisks, including his own original name Amenhotep IV and his father's name, Amenhotep III. They even entered tombs and erased the name. Akhenaten even extended the erasure to every occurrence of the plural of 'god' and to placenames that revered the gods, especially Amun, as far south as the fourth cataract in Nubia. This desecration may have been completely inspired by religious fervour, or an economic tool to ensure that all the revenue from the temples of Egypt was directed to the new city of the Aten, or it perhaps a combination of the two.

There is little doubt that the changes in the religion and the diversion of the revenue benefited the coffers of the king and his new city. The economy was clearly an issue in the religious revolution, as the boundary stela record officials as saying:

> May his Lordship govern from Akhetaten. May you conduct every land to him (*the Aten*). May you tax the towns and islands for him. Every city down to ... every ... belonging in its entirety to the Aten, in accordance with what he himself ordains ...[9]

It is highly unlikely that any official would sanction extra taxes to pay for the new city and new religion, but placing this request into a religious text – claiming the extra taxes were for the god – was a very clever act of propaganda to soften the blow of the diverted or inflated tax needed for the religious revolution.

Akhenaten's aggression, in particular to the cult of Amun, is understandable albeit overzealous; the cult of Amun was the richest and most powerful in Egypt throughout the earlier eighteenth dynasty until the reign of Amenhotep III. The destruction of the cult of Amun therefore ensured it neither equalled nor exceeded the power of the king.

Such desecration had never taken place before. It was acceptable to erase the names of kings of turbulent periods, pretending they had never existed, but not the names of the gods. No doubt this act was met with horror by all of Egypt. Even before the desecration of the temples and monuments there would have been opposition to the new religion (although Akhenaten does not report any) but, then again, kings rarely recorded negative aspects of their reigns. However, he clearly felt threatened and is often depicted surrounded by a personal bodyguard of numerous Asiatic and Nubian soldiers. Choosing a foreign bodyguard ensured greater safety, as not only were they not necessarily affected by his religious changes, but were also totally dependent on him for their livelihood.

The text on the boundary stelae hint at a problem in Thebes, which may have instigated the move. Akhenaten does not specify what this problem was but states he no longer wants to listen to the 'evil words', which is why he moved the capital. The boundary stela is thought to be a verbatim record of one of the king's speeches and gives an insight into his speaking style:

> It was worse than those things I heard in regnal year four,
> It was worse than those things I heard in regnal year three,
> It was worse than those things I heard in regnal year two,
> It was worse than those things I heard in regnal year one,

It was worse than those things Nebmaatre (*Amenhotep III*)
    heard,
It was worse than those things which ... heard,
It was worse than those things Menkheperure (*Thutmosis III*),
and it was worse than those things I heard by any kings who
    had ever assumed the White Crown (*rule of the south*).[10]

Whatever these 'things' were, they were bad enough to encourage
Akhenaten to leave Thebes and to bring the entire royal court and
religious community with him. Reeves suggests that this terrible
occurrence in Thebes may have been an attempt on his life by the
Amun priesthood or the followers of the Amun cult (which nar-
rows the assassin down to any of the Egyptian populus!), although
Monsterrat does not believe the priests or followers of Amun possessed enough power to threaten the life of the king and feels
another reason should be considered.[11] Whatever convinced
Akhenaten to move to a new city, he felt he had to hand-pick his
officials and fellow city-dwellers to ensure his safety.

Akhenaten's father and grandfather were both military kings
but it is often said that Akhenaten was a pacifist. This is belied
by the level of military presence at Akhetaten, especially in his
personal bodyguard – it could even be said that Akhetaten was a
military city. Akhenaten possessed the wealth of the temples, the
power of the throne and the military force necessary to enforce his
new beliefs, all of which he no doubt used ruthlessly, should
opposition be voiced in his Utopian city of the sun.

Of more direct relevance to the early years of Tutankhamun's
life were the palaces of Akhetaten. Akhenaten built at least four
palaces: the King's House, the Great Palace, the North Palace and
the North Riverside Palace. The North Riverside Palace was the
most northerly and consisted of a square tower enclosed within a
sizeable fortified wall with a large entrance gate.[12] In one of the
scenes of the royal procession, this palace is depicted as a fortified

building, indicating its function as protection for the king. The building was decorated with images of the royal family. Kemp believes this may have been the primary royal residence, although, sadly, archaeologically there is little left, due to the changing course of the Nile.[13] Between the enclosure wall and the palace were barrack-type apartments, which probably housed the royal body-guard and across the road were some of the largest houses in the city, homes to the top officials. To the north of the palace was a large administrative building, complete with granaries that provided the palace with food. The whole area is well protected but somewhat isolated, overlooked by the cliff. It was an ideal place for Akhenaten to live.[14] The King's Road started at this palace and ran south, towards the Central City and the other palaces and temples. The first palace on the southern journey was the North Palace.

The presence of his name on small finds within the building suggests Tutankhamun may have lived at the North Palace, which may have been home to the women and some of the royal children. Akhenaten and Nefertiti had six daughters: Meritaten, born at the start of Akhenaten's reign, Meketaten, their second daughter, Ankhesenepaten, the future wife of Tutankhamun, born in year five (1345 BCE), Neferneferuaten, born in year eight (1342 BCE) and Neferneferure, born in year nine (1341 BCE). The youngest daughter was Setepenre; she died in childhood. All may have lived, perhaps for only part of the year, at the North Palace. The temple is quite compact, indicating long-term or permanent use would be difficult but the palace could have been used as a temporary retreat.

It is clear that Nefertiti lived in the North Palace after her with-drawal from public life in year thirteen (1337 BCE) of Akhenaten's reign. There are also inscriptions that suggest Kiya, the secondary wife of Akhenaten, may also have lived there.[15] Later, it became the primary residence of Meritaten; her name is prominent at the site, quite clearly, a palace of the royal women. The evidence suggests that, for a short period at least, Nefertiti lived at this palace with her three youngest daughters Ankhesenepaten, Neferneferuaten and Neferneferure.[16] There are also attestations of Tutankhamun's name, indicating he lived here too. It is possible that Tutankhamun met his future wife, his half-sister Ankhesenepaten, at this palace, was brought up with her and no doubt played and perhaps was educated alongside her. She was some two years older than Tutankhamun and as his half-sister, may have looked after him and protected him.

The 'Children of the Kap' may also have lived there with the young prince.[17] These children were the offspring of foreign chieftains who were brought up with the Egyptian royal children. When they were later placed in control of their countries, they were expected to maintain loyalty to Egypt. At least two of these children, Heka-nefer and Khai, were later officials in the administration of Nubia under Tutankhamun. They were both called 'Children of the Kap' and were probably his childhood friends, and in daily contact with the young Tutankhamun.

The excavations at the North Palace, situated along the King's Road to the south of the North Riverside Palace and in a rather isolated spot, show there was a huge stone structure in the centre of the mud-brick screen wall which divided the entrance court from the sunken central court. The stone used for its construction was removed in antiquity but the gypsum foundations show the imprints of the stone blocks, setting-out lines and finger grooves along the edges of the stone courses, enabling a full outline of the building to be derived. Even the footprints of the ancient builders are still clearly visible. This stone building may have housed a 'Window of Appearances'.

Near the gateway and door jambs of the North Palace, gold leaf and paint fragments have survived, indicating the luxurious decoration that adorned Tutankhamun's childhood home. The central court had a sunken garden, separated by mud ridges into cubit-sized plots (approximately 50 cm), with a small well or shallow pool. The courtyard was surrounded by numerous chambers, each decorated with brightly coloured images of birds in papyrus thickets. One room clearly shows the whole wall was painted, with the bottom half representing water and the top half representing marshland. These small chambers had curtains for privacy and a bed-recess at the rear so the royal women and children could have an afternoon siesta when the sun became too hot.[18]

This garden pavilion was no doubt a very beautiful place to sit and relax on a sunny afternoon. One can imagine watching the dragonflies and butterflies land on the water plants and the breeze coming off the water, which no doubt would have held fish and possibly frogs. Perhaps, as a young boy, Tutankhamun played here with his wet-nurse, trailing his hand in the water and trying to catch the fish or collecting tadpoles to examine at close quarters later. There was also an aviary at the North Palace, which enabled the young children living there to observe nature at first hand and learn to identify the birds of Egypt.[19] Although the exact species kept in the aviary will never be known, it is likely to have held ibises, hawks, hoopoes and possibly even an ostrich, all species found in the surrounding desert. Ornamental gardens and pools such as these are often represented in Amarna art; the period is known for its realistic images of wildlife. The pavements and walls of the palaces were decorated with images from nature. Akhenaten may even have had a 'zoological garden' at the North Palace, filled with wild desert animals, including lions, wolves, jackals and maybe even imported monkeys, baboons, bears or giraffes. Perhaps Tutankhamun, as a small child living at Akhetaten, visited the zoo and learned about the animals that were housed there, which may have later developed into his love of animals – albeit a love of hunting them!

The King's Road continued southwards through the Central City, the administrative centre of Akhetaten. Dominating the end of this road were two palaces, joined by a bridge over the road. To the west was the Great Palace, the private quarters, and to the east, the public quarters, known as the King's House. The Great Palace stood by the side of the Nile and consisted of large columnated halls, with decorated floors and painted walls. One of these floors was discovered by Petrie in 1891. It was 76 square metres (250 square feet) in extent, made of plaster, painted with a lake and reeds with pin-tailed ducks flying in the air and calves kicking their heels on the ground. Although important as an example the Amarna artistic style, the floor also gives an idea of the size of the palace, as this floor belonged to just one room. Petrie was so enamoured of it that he applied to the Antiquities Service for a roof to be built over it to protect it. While he was waiting for this to be approved, he constructed a walkway for visitors over the floor, so they could view it without damaging it. For further protection he covered the whole floor with a thin, hand-applied layer of tapioca and water. Eventually, as he had requested, a shed was erected over it. Sadly, approximately twenty years later, the farmer who owned the surrounding land, tired of the hordes of tourists coming to see it, destroyed it one evening by shattering it to pieces with a hammer. The fragmentary remains are currently in the Egyptian Museum, Cairo – although very heavily restored.

The main columned hall of the palace led to six chambers, which have the remains of platforms and may have been the bedrooms of the six princesses. Next to each bedroom was a small room that may have been a playroom; a number of paint-brushes and pens stained with paint were discovered there and traces of paint marks on the walls may have been left by the little girls whilst playing.[20] There was a large screen facing the road, behind which was a courtyard, with colossal statues of Akhenaten, unseen to those outside the palace. This palace would also have housed a harem, or women's quarters, when the royal children were residing there, with a garden for the women to pass the time in. The layout of this garden is sadly lost to us, although we know it led to the Nile. There was probably a private harbour and landing stage, for deliveries to the palace and a place for the royal barge to drop anchor.[21] (Images of these boats can be found in the tomb of May (no. 14).) The garden may have provided a safe place for the children of the palace to learn to row, swim and fish under the watchful eyes of the servants and guards.

To the south of the private chambers was a small temple for the sole use of the royal family, meaning they could worship without having to leave the palace. Smenkhkare, as co-regent to Akhenaten, made a large addition to the Great Palace in later years, a columned hall, with 544 mud brick columns and wall-to-wall faience tiles, in which he could meet and greet his ministers and foreign envoys separate from Akhenaten's chambers.

A bridge led from the Great Palace to the King's House, east of the King's Road. The Window of Appearances, which dominates Amarna art, may have been on this bridge or may have been in the eastern palace. The King's House was the more public palace, where the king met his ministers and conducted the business of the city. The structure included magazines, stores, the palace, a courtyard, the police barracks of Mahu (the chief of police) and the Amarna Record Office (where the 'Amarna Letters' were discovered).

Although Tutankhamun may have lived in the northern part of the city, at the North Palace, it is likely that he occasionally spent time in the other palaces, either for state visits and displays, or in his role as heir to the throne. No doubt he accompanied his father Akhenaten and older brother Smenkhkare in the daily chariot processions and enjoyed the rest periods at the palaces and temples. One image from the restored plaster fragments of the North Palace shows an effeminate figure in a chariot, believed to be Smenkhkare, followed by a smaller chariot ridden by Tutankhamun, showing they took part.[22]

This idyllic image of the childhood of the royal children and the beautiful surroundings of the city was really just a clever façade. The city of Akhetaten was unusual, inhabited by carefully-chosen people, who all held office within the city and were aware that their future relied on a king absorbed in his own world. Many of the inhabitants clearly flattered the king, paying lip service to his god and worshipping their traditional gods in their homes. This duplicity would eventually give rise to anger, bitterness and retaliation. In the early years, before Tutankhamun was born, Akhetaten was a city of opportunity: those invited to live there would have the best of everything but as time went by this slowly changed. International relations were neglected and the increasing threat of the Hittites throughout the Near East left the inhabitants feeling vulnerable, for their ruler seemed uninterested in anything other than the Aten.

Tutankhamun and the rest of the royal children were protected from these feelings of animosity and uncertainty by their confinement to the palace and the well-planned processions through the street, where it was essential that the people showed pleasure in and respect for the royal family. The young prince was surrounded by high officials, who played an important role in his childhood and upbringing. Many officials came daily to the palaces, conversing with the king and controlling various aspects of the city and the palace. Amongst these palace-based officials were a number responsible for the protection of the harem and the royal children as well as those responsible for the education and military training of the children, plus a plethora of servants. Many of these officials remained dear to Tutankhamun and later in life he rewarded them with positions of power, showing they were influential during the formative years of the young king.

CHAPTER 3

A king is born

There is a lot of uncertainty about the early years of Tutankhamun's life, starting with his birth and parentage. The theories and ideas regarding his place of birth and early upbringing depend on the parentage of the young boy, which is something Egyptologists are unable to agree on. There seems to be little doubt that Tutankhamun was of royal blood, as his succession to the throne at such a young age indicates – it is unlikely that he would have been placed on the throne at nine years old if he was not the only surviving heir. Even if he were not of royal blood – a usurper – he could not have instigated the usurpation alone and it is unlikely that a more powerful person would put a child on the throne if that child did not have a legitimate claim.

Whoever his parents were, it is clear that Tutankhamun was born between years seven to nine (1343–41 BCE) of the reign of Akhenaten and was approximately nine years old when he ascended the throne, on the death of Smenkhkare in 1333 BCE. A decorated tunic, wrapped around the statue of Anubis in Tutankhamun's tomb (KV62) may give the date of his birth.[1] The tunic has red and blue stripes making the cloth appear purple; on the bottom hem the cartouche of Akhenaten is embroidered, indicating it was produced during his reign. The tunic is only suitable for a new-born baby and the date under the cartouches thus may be the year of Tutankhamun's birth; year seven of Akhenaten (1343 BCE). This tunic may have been worn by Tutankhamun at a naming ceremony, or some other ritual of royal infancy, at Akhetaten and kept as an heirloom from his childhood.

As the child was born at the height of the Aten cult, he was given the name Tutankhaten, which he changed to the more widely-known Tutankhamun on his ascension to the throne, to show his increasing recognition of the traditional gods, in particular Amun. This re-naming began the distancing of Tutankhamun from Akhenaten, the Amarna period and from his own parents. However, the evidence regarding his family is inconclusive and Egyptologists have a number of different theories.

Amenhotep III and Tiye: some believe Tutankhamun's parents were Amenhotep III and Tiye. Scholars who believe this also believe in the theory of a long co-regency between Amenhotep III and Akhenaten, as Tutankhamun was not born until year seven of Akhenaten's reign, year 33 of the reign of Amenhotep III (1343 BCE). If Amenhotep and Tiye were his parents, Tutankhamun may have been born at the palace of Malkata in Thebes, known as 'The splendour of the Aten', rather than at Akhetaten. There is evidence that he was at Malkata during Amenhotep III's reign.[2] However, it is uncertain whether this palace was a long-term residence or a ceremonial palace; if it were merely ceremonial, he may have been born elsewhere. However, even if he were Akhenaten's son, it is likely that Tutankhamun visited his grandfather's palace, so his presence there is not conclusive proof of parentage.

The main evidence for Amenhotep III as Tutankhamun's father is an inscription carved by Tutankhamun on one of Amenhotep III's stone lions, in the Nubian temple of Soleb, in which Tutankhamun refers to Amenhotep as 'father'. However this term was often used to denote any ancestors or forefathers and does not necessarily mean that Tutankhamun was the son of Amenhotep

III. When Tutankhamun carved this inscription he had begun the elimination and vilification of Akhenaten. As well as calling Amenhotep III his 'father', he also dated his regnal years starting from the end of Amenhotep III's reign; completely eliminating the Amarna years. This was a traditional political tool used by Egyptian kings; Horemheb did the same during his reign, also dating his regnal years from the end of the reign of Amenhotep III and thus eradicating Akhenaten, Smenkhkare, Tutankhamun and Ay from history. However, no one believes Horemheb to be the son of Amenhotep III, even though his parentage has also not been confirmed.

One thing that causes concern regarding Amenhotep III and Queen Tiye as Tutankhamun's parents is their age when he was born; Tiye was between forty-eight and fifty-two years old and it is therefore quite unlikely she was his mother.[3] Even in the modern world, it is rare for women to give birth in their fifties without medical assistance; in ancient Egypt the average age of death for a woman was thirty, so at fifty-two Tiye was elderly and unlikely to be fertile. If this was a rare case of a late pregnancy and childbirth the likelihood of it resulting in a healthy child would have been small and although Tutankhamun died young his mummy indicates he was healthy.

Even if Tiye was not Tutankhamun's mother, it is often stated that she was the mother of Smenkhkare, the accepted older brother of Tutankhamun, who followed Akhenaten on to the throne.

Amenhotep III and Sitamun: the theory that Amenhotep III was the father of Tutankhamun is more widely accepted than Tiye as his mother. Amenhotep III is known to have had a large harem with many secondary wives; some scholars believe Amenhotep and a secondary wife, perhaps even his daughter Sitamun, were Tutankhamun's parents. At approximately twenty-seven years old, Sitamun was of a suitable childbearing age in year seven (1343 BCE).

Figure 1 *Akhenaten, the father of Tutankhamun. Luxor Museum. Photograph courtesy of Geoff Webb.*

Akhenaten and Nefertiti: some scholars believe Tutankhamun was the son of Akhenaten (Figure 1) and his Great Royal Wife, Nefertiti (Figure 2), although the evidence again is not conclusive. Not all scholars are convinced, as Nefertiti is only ever depicted with her six daughters and it is often assumed she had no sons. However, in the eighteenth dynasty royal sons were rarely depicted in official inscriptions. They were normally only depicted on private monuments; either their own or those of the officials.[4] This suggests Nefertiti could have given birth to sons but protocol prevented them from being depicted alongside her. This theory is not watertight and is not widely accepted.

Figure 2 *Nefertiti, the stepmother of Tutankhamun. Ashmolean Museum, Oxford. Photograph courtesy of Wayne Frostick.*

Akhenaten is often portrayed as monogamous, whereas in reality he had a number of secondary wives who could have given birth to Tutankhamun, should Nefertiti not have been his mother. Akhenaten had at least four recorded wives: Nefertiti, Kiya, Tadukhipa (a Mitannian princess) and a Babylonian princess.[5] Akhenaten also married his daughter Ankhesenepaten (who later married Smenkhkare and Tutankhamun) and it is possible that they had a child, Ankhesenepaten Tasherit (The Younger), together.

Akhenaten and Kiya: one of Akhenaten's secondary wives, Kiya, is the most popular candidate for the mother of

Tutankhamun, although there is insufficient evidence to prove it. An inscription from a *talatat* block found at Hermopolis refers to Tutankhamun as the 'king's bodily son, his beloved'.[6] His mother is not named and the king, his 'father' is not identified but as the block originally stood in an Aten temple at Akhetaten, could strongly indicate the 'father' was Akhenaten.[7]

Further evidence of Akhenaten as father of Tutankhamun is found in the royal tomb at Amarna. There are two different funerary suites, each with a mourning scene. One shows the death of the princess Meketaten, daughter of Akhenaten and Nefertiti. The king and queen are shown standing by the funeral bier, alongside the vizier, as witnesses to the death. A new-born child is being carried away by a servant, perhaps indicating that Meketaten died in childbirth. In the other funerary suite a similar scene also shows a woman on a funerary bed, although she is unidentified. There is a birthing pergola in the scene and a child is also being carried from the room, again possibly indicating that this woman died in childbirth.[8] This woman is often identified as Kiya, and it is quite certain that one of the new-born children depicted was Tutankhamun. Although their identities are uncertain, it is obvious that the birth of these children was important. Even though they were not Nefertiti, the Great Royal Wife's, offspring, their birth was witnessed by the vizier, the king and the queen, as proof of identification should they ever become heir to the throne.

Another block from Hermopolis shows Akhenaten and Kiya (identified by a distinctive wig, longer at the front than at the back) standing or sitting together; his head overlaps hers, which sits slightly in front of his. Their close proximity shows that Kiya had been raised to a position of great importance. This revered status could only be because she provided the king with a male heir and was rewarded accordingly.[9] If she was promoted to this prominent position, she obviously did not die in childbirth, which causes a problem for the identification of the woman in the second mourning scene of the royal tomb, unless she was revered posthumously for providing a male heir to the throne.

There is doubt as to who Kiya actually was. It is often stated that she may have been the Mittannian Princess Tadukhipa, originally sent by her father for marriage to Amenhotep III but she instead married Akhenaten. Her father was initially reluctant to send her to Egypt, as he had not heard from his sister, sent for marriage to Amenhotep III some years previously:

> You want to marry my daughter but my sister, whom my father sent to you, is with you although no one has seen her of late, or knows if she is alive or dead ... you said to my messengers when your wives were together standing in front of you 'your lady is before you'. Now this messenger did not recognise her. Does my sister really look like this?[10]

He eventually agreed to send his daughter after he was paid a good 'bride price':

> My brother has enriched me ten times more than my father. My son-in-law is to be married in Thebes in the presence of the statue of the god.

Tadukhipa probably arrived in year 38 of Amenhotep III, year 12 (1338 BCE) of Akhenaten, shortly before Amenhotep's death. Because of his death, she was sent instead to Akhetaten to the harem of Akhenaten. It would be interesting to know if Tadukhipa's father was informed of the change of plan and if so, what his opinion was.

However, the theory of Kiya as Tutankhamun's mother is unlikely, as her late arrival does not tie in with Tutankhamun's date of birth. If Kiya was his mother, she would have needed to be in Akhetaten in year seven (1343 BCE), three years before the arrival of the Mitannian princess. If Akhenaten and Kiya were Tutankhamun's parents, he was probably born at Akhetaten, possibly in the North Palace, where his name is attested on small artefacts, indicating that at some point he lived here.

Smenkhkare and Meritaten: the final couple to be considered as parents of Tutankhamun are Smenkhkare and his Great Royal Wife and half-sister, Meritaten. Smenkhkare was co-regent with Akhenaten from year 14 (1336 BCE), when Tutankhamun was about seven years old. It is thought that the block discovered at Hermopolis, which states that Tutankhamun is the 'King's Son', could refer to Smenkhkare, although the block was originally inscribed before Smenkhkare's co-reign.

However, as Smenkhkare was probably only eleven years old when Tutankhamun was born, it is widely accepted that he was not his father but his brother. Smenkhkare was probably born before, or very shortly after, Akhenaten came to the throne. This raises the question as to why Akhenaten's sons were not mentioned in the surviving texts.

Smenkhkare was married to two of Akhenaten's daughters, Meritaten and Ankhesenepaten, (later the wife of Tutankhamun). However, Ankhesenepaten was also married to her father Akhenaten, indicating that she married Smenkhkare on the death of their father (in 1333 BCE), as she could not be married to two men at the same time.[11] When Akhenaten died, she married Smenkhkare and when he died (about six months later) she married Tutankhamun, only to be widowed again ten years on. If this were an Agatha Christie novel she would be given the title of 'Black Widow', or at least 'Unlucky' – especially for potential husbands. However, she was not the heroine of a novel but a young girl, clearly being used as a political pawn, married to the reigning king as a means of legitimisation, and to ensure she was not left single and attractive to men who might have ideas of usurping the throne through this particularly unstable period.

Regardless of who his parents were, Tutankhamun was no exception to the tradition that royal children were not brought up

Figure 3 *Tutankhamun and his wet-nurse Maia (after Zivie 1998). Illustration by Charlotte Booth.*

by their mothers and he was placed in the care of a wet-nurse in the royal harem. In ancient Egypt, it was common for children to be breast-fed for up to three years, as weaning was a particularly dangerous time in a child's life and breast milk was a way of providing safe nourishment. In 1997, the tomb of Tutankhamun's wet-nurse, Maia, was discovered, introducing us to a major influence of his formative years. Maia was buried in the necropolis at Saqqara (Figure 3). She held the titles 'Royal Nurse' and 'The one who has fed the god's body'; images within the tomb show her embracing the young king. He was obviously very fond of his nurse and it is clear that she survived until he came to the throne, as he endowed her with titles such as 'Highly favoured by the good god' and 'The one beloved of the Lord of the Two Lands'.[12] In her tomb, a dog is shown under her seat and the king upon her lap, indicating that a pet dog, whether hers or his, was a feature of his childhood.[13]

Reeves suggests that a wooden chair in Tutankhamun's tomb was the chair used by Maia while feeding the infant Tutankhamun.[14] However, the chair is very low, only 16.4 cm from the floor, with a flat wooden seat (approximately 36×25 cm) and a low back rest: too small to hold both an adult and child and it is therefore possible that it was only used by the young Tutankhamun, nonetheless, an important aspect of his childhood life at Amarna.[15] These low seats are often depicted in eighteenth dynasty tomb banquet scenes; the revellers sit with their knees to their chests, showing such chairs were part of the life of the rich and influential at this time.

Despite the uncertainty regarding the exact familial relations of Tutankhamun, it is clear from his tomb that he was a very family-oriented boy, although there is a degree of uncertainty as to how a funerary assemblage was put together; Tutankhamun might have started collecting objects from a young age or they might have been assembled after his death. It seems a number of items were donated, so the donor would be represented in the royal tomb but in the case of his family, many were long dead and therefore were unable to make the donation themselves. It is likely that, even if the goods were assembled after his death, with no personal choice, objects belonging to him and important to him were included along with traditional funerary goods, military items and food. Many of the items in his tomb may have belonged to him or at least been familiar to him.

Many objects in his tomb were inscribed for other members of the Amarnan household and may have held some meaning for him or would be thought useful for the afterlife. Many of the items belonging to his family members seem to have had no practical use to a young boy and therefore can be interpreted as treasured mementoes of those long-dead relatives. Egyptologists often look for complicated reasons as to why he would have a lock of Tiye's hair, Meritaten's palette and clappers (similar to castanets) and a vase of ointment bearing the name of Amenhotep III.[16] They seem loath to admit there could be an emotional tie to these objects; yet they must be in the tomb for a reason, albeit one that it is difficult to understand. Why can't it simply be that Tutankhamun kept these objects in an attempt to remember his stable early years, before death took his family away?

Among the heirlooms in the tomb are three musical instruments: a pair of clappers and two sistra. These instruments were traditionally used by women in the religious cults of Isis or Hathor and are unlikely to have belonged to Tutankhamun. They probably belonged to some of the many female members of his family. The pair of clappers were made of ivory, carved in the shape of human arms ending in hands. The emphasis on hands in Amarna art (normally seen at the end of rays emanating from the solar disc) made this an appropriate design for sacred instruments. They were nearly 16 cm long, with a hole in one end; they would have been strung together and the string looped over the hands of the women holding them, making clapping them together simple.[17] This pair of clappers was inscribed with the names of Queen Tiye and Princess Meritaten (the eldest daughter of Akhenaten and Nefertiti) who may have owned them: 'Great Royal Wife Tiye, Living Wife, King's Daughter Meritaten'. As Meritaten is titled 'Daughter of the reigning king', rather than as 'Wife of the king', this shows she owned them before she married Smenkhkare. The joining of her name with her grandmother's links them and indicates that, like Tutankhamun, Meritaten was family-oriented and wanted to honour her grandmother.[18] We do not know whether this honouring of her grandmother was done before or after her death in year 14 (1336 BCE), when Tutankhamun was seven years old. It was not unusual for clappers to be placed in a funerary context and it is possible that Tutankhamun acquired these instruments when the royal court was moved from Akhetaten to Thebes, which resulted in the re-burial, in the Valley of the Kings, of Smenkhkare and Tiye. Tutankhamun may have emptied their tombs in Akhetaten of funerary items and kept some for his own use. At this point, in the early years of his reign, he had lost all his family except Ay and Mutnodjmet and may have wanted to cling on to the last possessions of his beloved sister Meritaten.

Also in the tomb were two sistra (Plate 1); sacred rattles, gilt bronze arches threaded with snake-shape bars of the same material. At the end of each of these bronze bars were three square metallic discs, which hit against each other, rather like a modern tambourine. This created a tinkling sound that accompanied the rattling of the bars against the bronze arches. The arches were set into handles of gilded wood, normally formed of a Hathor head and shrine or, during the reign of Akhenaten, a flower.[19] However, the sistra in Tutankhamun's tomb were totally plain, with no artistic representations or inscriptions adorning them. They had been used, as shown by marks on the inside of the arches, so they were not unfinished funerary or votive offerings. As they were normally used only by women, we can assume they belonged to one of Tutankhamun's female relatives, although as they bear no name, we cannot be sure exactly who.[20] The list of female relatives to whom they might have belonged to is particularly long; as most of them died when Tutankhamun was young, he probably kept them in remembrance. They could have belonged to his grandmother, Tiye, who died when he was seven, his stepmother, Nefertiti, who died when he was six, his mother, Kiya, who may have died giving birth to him, or one of five half-sisters, all of whom died before he became king; all before he was nine years old.

No man would ever need these instruments, in life or death, so they were clearly relics or keepsakes of his past, a means for him to cling on to the stability of his childhood before he was thrown into the responsibility of kingship at a young age. During his early years he was surrounded by beloved women; to lose them when he needed them most was obviously a wrench. As these instruments were clearly from the Amarna period, it is unlikely that they were used in the traditional cults of Isis and Hathor. They may have been used in the cult of the Aten, perhaps at the Sunshade Temples, the temples of the royal women at Akhetaten.

A number of other heirlooms were also discovered in his tomb, representing belongings of many other of his family members:

Scarabs, a glass mandagora fruit and two calcite vessels belonging to Thutmosis III, an ancestor of a hundred years before;

Three calcite vessels of Amenhotep III and a joint vessel of Amenhotep III and Tiye, his grandparents;

A model adze belonging to Amenhotep III and Tiye, his grandparents;

A lock of hair in a small coffinette marked with the name of Queen Tiye;

A pectoral and a faience bangle belonging to his father Akhenaten, and two bangles belonging to Neferneferuaten (*Nefertiti*), his stepmother;

Sequins belonging to Ankheperure (*Smenkhkare*) and Meritaten, his brother and half-sister and sister-in-law;

A scribal palette of Meritaten, his half-sister;

A bow belonging to Ankheperure (*Smenkhkare*);

A whip stock inscribed with the name of Thutmosis (the king's son), who was Akhenaten's elder brother and Thutankhamun's uncle;

A number of boxes belonging to Neferneferure, his half-sister, Akhenaten, Neferneferuaten (Nefertiti) and Meritaten.[21]

These heirlooms give us some insights into Tutankhamun, the person. Having a lock of his grandmother's hair, his sister's palette, his grandfather's vessels and musical instruments belonging to one of his female family members is completely understandable in context. By the time he was nine years old, all his family, except his great uncle Ay, his step-aunt Mutnodjmet and his half-sister and wife Ankhesenamun had died, whether due to foul play, the 'Asiatic Illness' or plague. In the absence of photographs, these relics were a means of clinging to their memories and to memories of a happier time, when all he was concerned with was hunting and playing with the birds and fish in the pleasure pools of the palace. He was a young child, thrown into an adult world without the support of a loving family.

Tutankhamun spent the first seven to nine years of his life at the new city of Akhetaten, although it is uncertain whether he was born there. As the palaces of Malkata, Memphis and Gurob were still used throughout the reign of Akhenaten to house some of the royal women, it is possible he was born at one of them.[22] However, there is no evidence from any site to prove where he was born or where he spent his early years. There is evidence of his name at the North Palace, but unfortunately only on small artefacts rather than architectural elements, which suggest he was at least known there. It is likely that the six daughters of Nefertiti and Akhenaten, Tutankhamun's half-sisters, were also brought up in Akhetaten and he may have lived with the six princesses as well as other 'Children of the Kap'. They would have been close, creating the life-long attachments reflected, in later years, in Tutankhamun's choice of officials.

From a young age, Tutankhamun received a traditional royal education, preparing him for a life in the army, the administration or the priesthood, should he not become king. This ensured he was educated in reading, writing and military skills. It is quite clear that Tutankhamun was literate and may even have excelled at his studies. In his tomb were fifteen scribal palettes, of different sizes, including portable ones, some bearing traces of partly-used inks. A golden reed holder (the ancient equivalent of a pencil case) indicates he received at least a basic education in reading and writing in one of the palaces of Akhetaten. If his education did not take place at the North Palace, it is possible it happened at the 'House of Life', a learning institution and archive near the Royal Record Office and within the enclosure of the King's House.

One palette was inscribed with the name of Meritaten and another with the name of Meketaten; both mementos of his half-sisters. Another palette, made of ivory, belonged to his grand-father, Amenhotep III.[23] Meritaten's palette (Plate 2) was obviously a treasured object; it was placed between the paws of the Anubis statue in the treasury of his tomb, a position of great religious significance. One of the palettes was an artist's palette, with indentations to hold six different colours, showing Tutankhamun may have tried his hand at drawing and painting, whether as a small child or as a teenager. Tutankhamun seems to have been a bright child, who showed an interest in many topics, which no doubt pleased his tutors, one of whom is thought to have been Ay, his great uncle.

The presence in his tomb of a papyrus-burnishing tool raises questions about his abilities and knowledge. If it did belong to him, does that mean he could make papyrus as well as write on it? Possibly, like other children, he asked about how papyrus was made but it is likely that if, as king, he enquired about something it would be explained in the most elaborate way and by practical demonstration. It was doubtless a more thorough demonstration than the average tourist in Egypt gets when visiting the papyrus factories. The papyrus stalks were sliced horizontally and the outer green rind discarded (though no doubt used for something else). The inner pulp was sliced and laid in tidy rows and then another layer placed at right-angles on top of it. A pile of stones, or other weights, was placed on top of the sheets. As the moisture in the pulp evaporated, the two layers were firmly stuck together, then the surface of the finished sheet of papyrus was burnished using a special tool. The young Tutankhamun may have made his own paper, although how long this hobby lasted will remain unknown. His burnishing tool, made of ivory and with a decorated handle, would have enabled him to complete his paper professionally.[24] It is endearing to imagine the child-king making his own paper, then sitting quietly, carefully writing a letter or painting a picture and later presenting it to his sister/wife or one of the officials of the court who were concerned with his upbringing; Ay, Horemheb or Maia his wet-nurse. Unfortunately, this can only be conjecture, based on the presence of a rather unusual tool in his tomb. It is sometimes simpler to dismiss such items as donations from the stores, rather than try to work out why he had such an unusual item. It is not impossible that the young boy learned to make his own paper, in the same way that it is not impossible that he was literate or could ride a chariot, assumptions based on other objects found in his tomb.

Tutankhamun also expressed an interest in astronomy and perhaps the past. When he was king, he commissioned the repair of an astronomical instrument dedicated to the memory of his ancestor Thutmosis IV.[25] He never met this king, so possibly learned about him from his family when he was growing up, and wanted to acknowledge this eminent ancestor. The astronomical instrument was made of ebony ($2.69 \times 2.8 \times 1.5$ cm) and is inscribed:

> The kindly god made it with his two hands for his father Amun who placed him on his throne, even the King of Upper and Lower Egypt Nebkheperure, the Son of Re, Tutankhamun Ruler of Southern Heliopolis, restoring the monument of his father, King of Upper and Lower Egypt Menkheperure, the son of Re Thutmosis IV given life like Re for ever and ever.[26]

It is thought that the astronomical instrument may have originated in the tomb of Thutmosis IV, which was robbed in antiquity. It might have later have fallen into Tutankhamun's hands, inspiring him to restore it. Perhaps Tutankhamun recognised it for what it was and as part of his education had learned how to use such a device. The instrument was used to determine the meridian time, so the water clocks could be set, especially at night, using the instrument's twenty-four divisions, which represented the hours of the day and night.[27] When this instrument came to his attention, whether or not he knew how to use it, he was sufficiently interested to restore it, rather than a more monumental object or structure. His interest in the past is attested by the existence of a number of objects in his tomb belonging to Thutmosis III, an ancestor of even greater antiquity. He was probably told stories of the military prowess of this king, giving him a masculine role-model that may not have been present in his father.

An important part of Tutankhamun's traditional royal education was the arts of warfare and charioteering. He seemed to have enjoyed this bit of his education; it sparked his passion for hunting and brought him one step closer to his military ancestor, Thutmosis III. In his tomb were four well-used hunting chariots, light Egyptian chariots with six-spoke wheels, made of bent wood and leather.[28] A fly-whisk (Plate 3) and three whip stocks were found with the chariots. One stock was made of ivory mounted in gold, electrum and silver and inscribed 'Who appears upon his team of horses as when Re ascends', likening the king in his chariot to the sun-god. A second stock was made of gilded wood, with a bronze tip and a marbled glass knob and inscribed 'The king's son, the troop commander, Thutmosis, who repeats life'. This stock had belonged either to a son of Thutmosis IV, a younger brother of Amenhotep III, or to the elder brother of Akhenaten who died young.

A golden fan, discovered between the third and fourth shrines in the burial chamber, bore scenes of Tutankhamun hunting ostrich in the desert. If this scene is to be believed, he was quite a talented hunter as it shows he had struck two of these large birds with his bow. Another image, from reused *talatat* blocks from the ninth pylon at Karnak, shows Tutankhamun participating in a lion and bull hunt. As a young boy, Tutankhamun was not strong enough to hunt wild lion alone and it is probable that the hunts, at least when he was very young, were set up to indulge his hobby. The animals were probably trapped before the king rode out in his chariot and held in an enclosure to make shooting easier. As he got older and his skills increased, he was able to try hunting in the desert, possibly escorted by his military leader, Horemheb. These stereotypical images were also tools to show the prowess of the king and indicate he was able to control chaos. However, hunting scenes are a common feature of the art of this king and numerous items in his tomb indicate that hunting was perhaps his favourite pastime.

Although the images of Tutankhamun hunting are quite stylised, the used chariots in his tomb and other riding and hunting paraphernalia indicate he knew how to ride, although quite how skilled he was remains unknown. A number of pairs of gloves and some gauntlets of unusual design were also placed in his tomb. The gloves have five fingers (Plate 4), whereas the gauntlets are separated into two fingers, with the thumb left free. These gauntlets were primarily used for charioteering (Plate 5). They are of varying sizes; Tutankhamun obviously owned some of the smaller pairs when he was a child, indicating he learned to ride a chariot while still young. Gauntlets were more ceremonial than ordinary gloves and may have been worn in public displays, such as the daily processions of Akhenaten and Nefertiti through the streets of Akhetaten. There are scenes of the young princesses, in miniature chariots, accompanying their parents in the daily processions. It is quite likely that the sons of the king, Smenkhkare and Tutankhamun, also accompanied the royal family on these jaunts.

There were also two ceremonial chariots, covered with gold leaf and decorated in embossed relief with traditional images of bound captives and the symbol of the unification of Egypt, showing that the king was the king of Upper and Lower Egypt. These chariots are unlikely ever to have been ridden, as the wheels were covered in gold leaf; using the chariots would have severely damaged them.

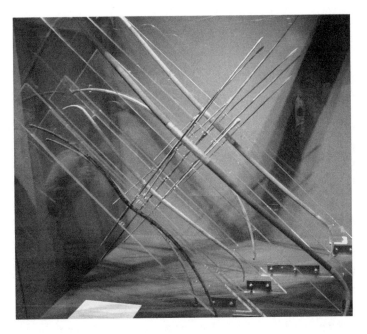

Figure 4 *Composite and self bows of Tutankhamun. Luxor Museum. Photograph courtesy of Wayne Frostick.*

Therefore it is likely they were created for his tomb and did not feature in the life of the young king.

A number of childhood objects in his tomb, including sling shots, bows and arrows (Figure 4) and scimitar swords, suggest Tutankhamun was trained in various hunting skills as a child. We have to consider whether a five year old child in ancient Egypt had similar play patterns to a modern five year old – and whether we would give a five year old a slingshot to play with – imagine the havoc he could have caused in the palace, pleasure pools and zoological gardens. The skills Tutankhamun learned in hunting were useful in his political life and the battles he later participated in. Both warfare and hunting were traditionally carried out with bows, arrows, spears or throw sticks and this early training would have prepared him for this.

A statue in the tomb depicts Tutankhamun hunting on a papyrus skiff, something which may have been part of his training and education. Papyrus skiffs were small vessels, made of bundles of papyrus reeds tied together. The cellular structure of the inner pith of papyrus, with hundreds of tiny air pockets, makes it buoyant but despite this buoyancy, the skiffs still filled with water, meaning whoever stood within got their feet wet.[29] Although no boat of this type was discovered in the tomb, many throw-sticks were, suggesting that hunting birds in the marshes was a pastime of the king. The skiff was the best form of transport in marshlands. Due to the flimsiness of the boats, learning to swim was also a necessity; we can assume the young boy was able to swim. The throw-sticks in his tomb were made of a variety of hardwoods; there was even a pair made of electrum – probably ceremonial examples which were never used. Many of the wooden throw-sticks were decorated with fragments of birch bark and one with the iridescent wings of beetles which gave a lovely, if somewhat unusual, finish.[30]

Further evidence of Tutankhamun's passion for hunting is found elsewhere. On the Giza plateau, very close to the Sphinx, the remains of a hunting lodge dating to the reign of Tutankhamun were uncovered in the 1920s by the archaeologist Baraize. This find was never announced; the lodge was promptly removed to reach the earlier remains beneath. The lodge was built on loose sand, three metres above the rock floor and behind the Khafre Valley Temple. The rectangular (13 × 35 metres) main structure was of mud brick, with limestone door-lintels, one inscribed with the name of Tutankhamun and his queen, identifying the structure as his. It is recorded that the structure contained a bath for the young king to wash away the dirt of a day's hunting. The water was removed from the bath through limestone drains which drained into a basin of limestone sunk into the floor. The structure had

eleven rooms flanking a central wall and was entered by two gate-
ways at the eastern end.[31] Although elaborate, it was likely to have
been a temporary rest house for royal visits, whether to hunt for
wild lions on the desert plateau or to make pilgrimage visits to the
nearby Sphinx, which was worshipped as the solar god,
Horemakhet.[32] This hunting lodge is very similar to one at Kom el
'Abd near Malkata in Luxor, built for his grandfather Amenhotep
III; perhaps Tutankhamun borrowed the idea from him.

However, the rest house at Kom el 'Abd was situated on a desert
plain, very close to a straight road and had a very different function.
The desert road starts about two kilometres from the edge of the
desert and runs in a straight line to the base of the hills at Kola el-
Hamra, 4.1 km away. The road is about 120 m wide and was hand-
cleared of all large stones. It is clear that this road did not lead
anywhere and must have had another purpose. The rest house is
believed to have been used by the king when he was chariot racing.
The remains consist of a rectangular platform (45×40 metres) of
mud brick with seven small houses upon it. The platform was
reached by a broad ramp that ended in a square landing. Four of the
houses formed a single block with a central corridor and have identical plans: an entrance chamber and an intermediate chamber
connecting it to the square living room, which had two smaller
chambers opening from one side. The two separate houses follow
the same plan, except that the intermediate chamber becomes a
third chamber leading from the living room. The seventh house is
larger and resembles an Amarna villa. These houses may have been
the caretakers' accomodation; in the centre of the platform a square
brick room, neither aligned nor centred, may have been a guard post
when the structure was not in use. Kemp believes the king stayed in
a tent on the platform for these racing visits.[33]

It is possible that young Tutankhamun travelled to Thebes to
witness his grandfather win the chariot races at Kom el 'Abd.
Imagine the excitement of staying in a tent on a high platform and

watching the chariots thunder down the road to the finishing line, amid a huge cloud of dust. The atmosphere on the platform was doubtless celebratory; Tutankhamun may have regarded them as happy times that he wanted to re-create in his own hunting lodge. As king, his passion was hunting rather than chariot racing, but he may have wanted to erect a similar lodge in memory of his child-hood. These lodges would also have provided an escape from the pressures of kingship and allowed the king to relax with his friends and indulge in his favourite pastime.

Such temporary encampments were probably more common than the archaeological record indicates. Kings travelled the length and breadth of Egypt for various expeditions: hunting, political or religious. In the larger cities, there were palaces which contained all the luxuries of home. There were palaces at Memphis and Luxor for religious and state visits, and at Gurob for hunting trips to the Faiyum. For less-visited sites, or those in out-of-the-way places, temporary camps like Kom el 'Abd and the Giza lodge held rudi-mentary comfort for shorter visits. There also seems to have been a third type of encampment: tents pitched in the desert. On one of the boundary stelae at Amarna it is stated that when Akhenaten was searching for his perfect city he stayed in a 'carpeted tent made for his majesty in Akhetaten, the name of which was 'Aten is Content''.[34] This tent was probably very similar to a military tent, with poles with decorated tops, draped with fabric or leather and a door within a wooden frame. This type of tent is depicted in the Memphite tomb of Horemheb and may have been similar to the canopy frame over the shrines in the tomb of Tutankhamun. The records of Thutmosis III's battle of Megiddo mention seven tent poles of silver taken from the prince of Kadesh, which probably refers to the military tent of the Hittite prince. The tent fabric, usually linen for military tents, was laid over the poles; Akhenaten probably had something more heavyweight for his stay in the desert, perhaps a canopy of reed matting or wool.[35]

Tutankhamun may have used such tents when hunting further afield than the Giza plateau. As two of the examples (pictorial and archaeological) of these military tents are dated to his reign (his canopy and the tent depicted in Horemheb's tomb), this indicates he had access to them when he needed to, although it is likely that his tent may have had gilded poles or a decorated canopy to reflect his royal status. Evidence suggests that Tutankhamun travelled to the marshes of the Faiyum to hunt. The Faiyum had been a popular place for royal hunting from as early as 1900 BCE. At the start of the eighteenth dynasty, a new royal harem, the *mi-wr*, was constructed at the town of Gurob in the Faiyum, which required a large staff, including farmers for the attached agricultural land.[36] Inscriptions from this harem indicate that Ankhesenamun spent some time here, possibly when Tutankhamun was hunting nearby; an image on the small golden shrine in his tomb shows Ankhesenamun handing arrows to her husband in the marshes, indicating she may have accompanied him (Plate 6).[37] We do not know how many of Tutankhamun's other wives were housed here either permanently or temporarily. In fact, we do not know how many other wives he had, but as a traditional king it was essential that he had an heir and a greater number of wives increased his chances of having sons.

For these jaunts into desert or marshland, Tutankhamun needed survival skills. The presence of a fire drill in his tomb suggest this was part of his royal education (Figure 5). Being able to use a fire drill ensured that when hunting, he was able to light a fire to keep warm in the cold desert evenings; although in reality he was accompanied on these excursions by servants and guards. There was also a walking stick, made of reed and set into a gold handle, inscribed 'a reed which his majesty cut with his own hand', indicating that he was taught how to carve using a sharp tool, either a copper or flint knife. He was obviously proud of this achievement, hence the reed was placed into his tomb, albeit alongside 130

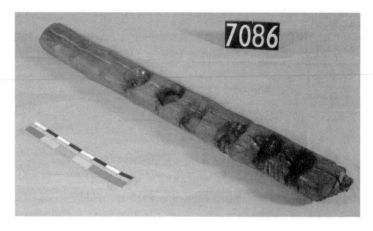

Figure 5 *Fire drill similar to the example found in Tutankhamun's tomb. Petrie Museum. Photograph courtesy of the Petrie Museum, UC 7086.*

others. Perhaps this stick was set into a handle as an indulgence to a young prince, as a means of encouraging him and keeping him happy, or perhaps it was a sign of genuine admiration for the young boy's talents.

The presence of such large numbers of sticks in his tomb has led to long academic debate about whether Tutankhamun needed these sticks for support when walking. Images of him from his tomb show him leaning against a staff; it was considered he may have had some disorder with his leg that resulted in a disability. Early X-rays of his mummy showed a curvature of the spine that could have resulted in a limp and necessitated the constant use of a stick. However, a CT (Computerised Tomography) scan carried out in 2005 discovered neither any natural disorder nor injury to his legs; the spine curvature was caused by the embalmers not laying the body straight before wrapping. Tutankhamun may have owned the sticks as a sign of status or even because they were fun objects to collect.

The prince's upbringing was not entirely fun-oriented. When he was not learning battle and hunting skills he participated in the ceremonial activities of the royal family at Akhetaten. The most documented rituals were the daily processions through the streets of the city but as a son and potential heir to the throne he probably participated in many more. Evidence from his tomb indicates that Tutankhamun may have participated in, or at least been present during one of Akhenaten's *heb sed* at Akhetaten. Akhenaten had more reasons than the average king to perform this festival before his thirty-year anniversary. The festival was an opportunity for the people to have a large feast, with extra food rations and a few days off work endearing an unpopular king to them.

The *heb sed* tunic from Tutankhamun's tomb, decorated with embroidery, was designed for a child and must have been worn by him when he was still living at Akhetaten. It is decorated with embroidered rosettes with golden centres and Maltese crosses. The collar has several rows of beads and the hem has repeated appliquéd *heb sed* hieroglyphic signs. This garment was probably made as a ceremonial outfit for Tutankhamun to wear at the second *heb sed* of Akhenaten, which took place some time after year seven and the birth of the young prince. Such a great public celebration would warrant the production of ceremonial clothes and was a perfect opportunity for the young prince to be paraded before the people of Akhetaten, displaying Akhenaten's virility and the continuance of the dynasty.

Other ceremonial clothes in the tomb indicate that Tutankhamun acted as a *sem* priest for the burial of his predecessor, although for Akhenaten or Smenkhkare is not certain. *Sem* priests carried out the rites and rituals on the body before burial, as well as prayer recitations, water sprinkling, lighting of incense and the 'Opening of the Mouth' ceremony. This ceremony was particularly important, as it ensured that the deceased was able to breathe, eat and speak in the afterlife. The *sem* priest was traditionally the deceased's eldest son; this ensured the line of succession, especially in the case of royalty, was clear. In traditional art, the *sem* priest is identified by a leopard-print cloak draped over his shoulder. Tutankhamun possessed three leopard cloaks; two of linen elaborately decorated with circles of red and blue with golden stars stitched on the circles to give the appearance of leopard spots and lined with a linen sheet. The third cloak was of real leopard skin, decorated with gold rosettes, discs and stars. The head of the leopard had been removed, as the full pelt was too big to be worn by a child as young as Tutankhamun, only nine or ten years old at the time. Attached to all three cloaks were wooden leopard heads, covered in gesso and gilded, the eyes inlaid with blue glass and crystal and with facial markings in blue glass. Four fake paws were cut into the pelt, with silver claws inserted, used to fasten the cloak at the shoulder. These skins appear to have been made for a small child and were probably designed for the 'Opening of the Mouth' ceremony, which was essential for the survival for the deceased in the afterlife. During his early years on the throne, Tutankhamun reburied Smenkhkare and possibly his grandmother, Tiye, in the Valley of the Kings and he may have worn these cloaks at the reburials. However we do not know if he had a specific role in these funerals, other than commissioning them and it is quite likely that he wore the ceremonial clothes, even if he did not perform the rituals.

When Tutankhamun was not participating in ceremonial events, or at school, he passed the time in a variety of ways. One of his favourite indoor pastimes was playing *senet*, a game of strategy rather like backgammon, played between two players. It was a very popular Egyptian board game; its name means 'Game of Passing'. It was played on grids of thirty squares (known as houses). The grid could be scratched on stone or carved on elaborate boards; three rows of ten squares, with five squares decorated with hieroglyphs. The players had an odd number of pieces, called 'dancers', each (five or seven were the norm). The number of squares moved was determined by 'throw sticks' or 'knuckle-bones'; wooden sticks with one plain and one painted side – the combination thrown determined the number of squares to be moved. Senet was played almost continually from around 2500 BCE and was depicted regularly in tombs, although in the eighteenth dynasty it changed from an everyday activity to a funerary one. The deceased are often shown playing senet with no opponent, symbolising the Fate they needed to beat to enter the afterlife.[38] There were different boards for everyday life and for the tomb. One of the senet sets from the tomb of Tutankhamun was clearly modified for the tomb, as it has long feline-footed legs and is mounted on a sledge of the type used to pull the sarcophagus to the tomb.

Four senet sets were found in the tomb of Tutankhamun, varying in size and including a portable set, indicating he was a keen player (Plate 7). Tutankhamun's boards were double-sided, for playing two different board games; a board of thirty squares for *senet* and a board of twenty squares for a game called 'robbers'. Sadly, the exact rules for playing either game are unknown and we can only guess at the details. It is suggested that *senet* was a more traditional game; hence it was on the bottom of the sets, with the 'robbers' game on top, indicating this was the more popular of the two.[39] All four sets have drawers in which to store the pieces, although whether the young prince put the pieces away himself or a servant cleared up after he had finished playing is open to question. One set is of particular interest in the life of Tutankhamun and is one that he may have used to play with his wife. The gaming board was of solid ivory and was found in a wooden chest with many compartments and Carter comments: 'From the contents ... that were found in the chest it becomes obvious that the chest was made for the knick knacks of a boy'.[40] This box is particularly small and was portable, easily transported from room to room in the palace, from city to city and on excursions to the hunting lodge. On the end of this box is a roughly carved image of the king and queen facing each other; Tutankhamun is seated and Ankhesenamun stands before him holding a lotus flower to his nose. The cartouches above their heads identify them as king and queen and therefore date either to the last two years at Amarna or the eight years during which they lived at Thebes and Memphis (Figure 6). Completing the set were two ivory knuckle-bones, five red ivory 'dancers' and five white ivory 'dancers', making up a set of ten. This box is the only one that has personal touches and perhaps gives us an insight into the people who once agonised over the next move or waited in anticipation to see how many squares the 'knuckle bones' would dictate could be moved. We can imagine the young king, aged nine or ten, playing his sister/wife, older than him by two years, at this game of strategy. Was she better at it than he? If he lost did he have a tantrum, or was he a graceful loser willing to learn from his mistakes? Was Ankhesenamun prepared to teach him how to move the pieces and how to trap his opponent? These

Figure 6 *Tutankhamun and Ankhesenamun; from the end of their portable senet set. Drawing by the author after Tait 1982 pl. xxiv.*

questions must remain unanswered, but when looking at this small object, the hours of fun they inevitably had playing it can almost be grasped from the pieces themselves.

There is little doubt that the early years of Tutankhamun's life were busy, fun and happy, despite the instability witnessed in the rest of Egypt due to the religious changes made by his father. However, in year 12 of Akhenaten's reign (1338 BCE) the decline of this stable life started and the young prince's world changed. In that year, Amenhotep III, Tutankhamun's grandfather, died, starting a long sequence of royal deaths, which have been attributed to a plague sweeping Akhetaten. In year 13 (1337 BCE) Nefertiti disappears from the records and possibly died. She seems to have been replaced on the throne by the new-co-regent Neferneferuaten, probably only twelve to fifteen years old when he came to the throne, who changed his name in year 14 (1336 BCE) to Smenkhkare. Tutankhamun was only about five when Nefertiti died and probably knew Smenkhkare well, despite the age difference, as they may have been brought up together. However, whether Tutankhamun understood what was happening regarding the throne of Egypt is anyone's guess. Smenkhkare ruled alongside Akhenaten until his death three years later (1336–1333 BCE). As he built a small temple at Memphis dedicated to the Aten, it is thought that Akhenaten may have named him co-regent to spread the cult of the Aten outside of Akhetaten. Akhenaten appears to have stayed at Akhetaten, creating what he believed was a strong religious base; he may have thought that sending his young co-regent out of Akhetaten would regain some of the power lost throughout Egypt.[41] However, the extension of the Great Palace at Akhetaten, intended for Smenkhkare's official use, indicates that he lived in Akhetaten and any excursions out of the city were temporary.

There has been much discussion as to the identity of Smenkhkare, as he does not appear in any of the records prior to his co-regency in year 14 (1336 BCE). Some believe he was

Akhenaten's homosexual lover and caused the collapse of Akhenaten's and Nefertiti's marriage.[42] There is no firm evidence to support this theory; it is more widely accepted that Smenkhkare was Akhenaten's son by a secondary wife and therefore the half-brother of Tutankhamun. This sibling relationship is further supported by the body discovered in tomb KV55. KV55, situated in the Valley of the Kings, was found sealed with Tutankhamun's seal and created a great deal of excitement in the Egyptological world. A number of items inside belonged to Queen Tiye and it was thought this may have been her tomb. The body was placed in a female coffin that had been adapted to befit that of a king, although the inscriptions identifying the owner had been hacked out. The body, believed at the time of discovery to be that of the aged dowager queen, was sent for analysis. Some scholars, despite close anatomical analysis to the contrary, still believe that the body is female, either that of Tiye or Kiya.[43] The anatomical analysis identified the body as a small-boned and wide-hipped male in his twenties or thirties, and was initially identified as either Akhenaten or Smenkhkare.[44] However, Akhenaten was older when he died leaving Smenkhkare as the only suitable candidate for the body. Further examination of the KV55 body (possibly Smenkhkare) and Tutankhamun proved they have the same skull morphology and the same blood group (type A2 MN), indicating they were related. This is the same blood group as that of Tuya, the grandmother of Akhenaten and shows a relationship between Tutankhamun, Smenkhkare and her.[45] However, it is not a rare group and the similarities could be coincidental. For a number of years Tutankhamun's skull shape caused some speculation, as in profile it appears to be greatly elongated. It was thought this was proof of a medical condition such as hydrocephalus or evidence of artificial head deformation. However, the 2005 CT scan of Tutankhamun indicated that the elongation of his head was within the normal variation of skull shapes and sizes.

Until clearer information regarding the origins of Smenkhkare is available the true familial relationship between Tutankhamun and he will remain uncertain, although it is generally accepted that they were brothers. This would go some way to explain why he was named co-regent; as the eldest son of Akhenaten, this would have been a traditional means of identifying the successor to the throne. Regardless of who he was, his untimely death in his twenties, after only three years of co-ruling and possibly six months of sole rule after the death of Akhenaten, spelt the end of the cult of the Aten. All the main protagonists had died: Amenhotep III in year 12 (1238 BCE), Nefertiti in year 13 (1337 BCE), Tiye and Princess Meketaten in year 14 (1336 BCE), Akhenaten in year 17 (1333 BCE) and later the same year, Smenkhkare. At his death, Smenkhkare's wife Meritaten also disappears from the records and it is likely that she died as well.

It has been suggested that as both Smenkhkare and Meritaten were young, only in their late teens or early twenties, they may have been murdered to leave the throne free for Tutankhamun.[46] However, their deaths must be added to a long list of royal deaths between year 12 to 17 (1238–1333 BCE). The most universally accepted theory regarding these deaths is that an epidemic, known as the 'Asiatic Illness', swept Akhetaten (and perhaps greater Egypt). This could account for the many deaths which took place in a few years. In the London Medical Papyrus the symptoms are described as: 'the body is coal black with charcoal spots in addition to the water (*urine*) as red liquid'. A recent study of fossilised insect remains at Tell el Amarna, carried out by Eva Panagiotakopulu a paleoentomologist from Sheffield University (UK), shows the presence of bedbugs, fleas and flies, as well as very cramped and crowded living quarters with questionable hygiene.[47] She suggests that the Nile Rat may have carried the flea responsible for bubonic plague, which then came into contact with the Black Rat (both present in Egypt at this time), which spread this infection worldwide. Perhaps further studies will pinpoint whether this epidemic in Amarna was an early case of the bubonic plague.

This Amarnan plague or epidemic is recorded by the Hittites as spreading from Egypt to Hattusha (the Hittite capital), following the capture of some Egyptian prisoners. This plague was highly contagious and not only affected the royal family but many others in Akhetaten. Many of the bodies were not buried here but were shipped to other villages in Egypt for traditional burials, so the extent of the epidemic cannot truly be quantified. In 2006, a cemetery of poor burials was uncovered at Akhetaten, showing that hundreds of people were buried there. However, early studies have not yet identified the cause of death, although it appears from the skeletal remains that they led short and difficult lives, consistent with a plague-ridden city rather than the glorious Utopia that Akhenaten was hoping to create.[48] The spread of this epidemic was primarily due to squalid living conditions, something totally unexpected in a new and economically strong city, but it was clearly contagious enough to spread to the royal family, who were the richest and cleanest in the city. The ordinary people doubtless viewed this epidemic as punishment for Akhenaten's abandoning of the traditional gods, and welcomed their reinstatement.

These eight family deaths must have affected the young prince Tutankhamun, who was only three or four years old when the deaths started. He watched his loved ones die slowly, and from a painful and unpleasant illness. He probably did not understand why his world was changing so much. The inhabitants of the city of Akhetaten were pressing for aid in their time of need, and for the numerous expensive burials. Funerals in ancient Egypt, for the people and royalty alike, were elaborate affairs, including the mummification and wrapping of the bodies in hundreds of metres of linen, elaborately decorated tombs and numerous goods placed in the burial chamber. A procession wound from the embalmers to the tomb, with the funerary goods, displaying the family's wealth, carried by servants and a group of female mourners paid to wail, throw dust over themselves and tear their clothes in grief. The wealthier the individual, the more mourners were needed to make a suitable display. The services of a *sem* priest were also required to carry out the religious ceremonies designed to aid the deceased in the afterlife. All these funerary needs would have affected the economy of Akhetaten, if there were an unusual number of deaths per family as a consequence of the plague. The depressing wails and sounds of grief from the city funerals would have drifted to the palace and mingled with the grief suffered from deaths within the palace, which continued for over five years. Between the ages of four and nine, Tutankhamun lived amidst grief and mourning. Within the palace, there was additional fear, as family members, one by one, fell ill and slowly died. Perhaps the children were kept in isolation to try and prevent the plague from spreading, meaning Tutankhamun may not have had the opportunity to say goodbye to his dying relatives and probably did not fully understand why he could no longer visit them. While suffering from this isolation, grief, miscomprehension and fear, the death of Smenkhkare was confirmed and the young prince was given yet more shocking news. He was now king, a scenario that may not have been expected by anyone, least of all the young boy himself.

CHAPTER 4

Ascent to the throne

The coronation of any new king was an elaborate affair, greeted with great anticipation and apprehension by the populus. In Tutankhamun's case, there would be a certain element of apprehension, as the people were probably unsure what their new boy-king could offer Egypt.

Since the time of Narmer (3100 BCE), coronations had traditionally taken place in Memphis, to reassert the traditional religion. However, it is likely there was also a ceremony at Thebes, at the temple of Karnak, indicating the re-establishment of the Amun cult. This dual ceremony showed the new king, Tutankhamun, was king of Upper and Lower Egypt. The temple of Karnak probably needed some quick repairs, as it had been neglected by Akhenaten for a number of years before the destruction of the name of Amun started in year nine (1341 BCE). Coronation ceremonies were accompanied by long processions through the streets; crowds of people watched the dancers, musicians, the military parade and possibly even a tributary parade from foreign peoples loyal to Egypt, bringing their nations' resources. The ceremony was carried out in the temple in the presence of traditional gods, such as Horus, Amun and Atum, the creator (Figure 7); new and unfamiliar deities to a young boy raised in the city of the Aten.

Figure 7 *Tutankhamun (or Horemheb) as Atum. Alexandria National Museum. Photograph courtesy of author.*

Meeting these unfamiliar deities would have been daunting and terrifying – the strange, animal-headed gods resembled nothing he had ever seen at Akhetaten.

One of the most important rituals of the coronation was the crowning, symbolically carried out by Amun. Tutankhamun was crowned with the numerous crowns of Egypt (Figure 8), representing all the roles that the king needed to play:

The Red crown of Upper Egypt
The White crown of Lower Egypt
The *Pasekhemty* (of combined crown of Upper & Lower Egypt)
The *Atef* crown of the sun-god Re
The *Seshed* headband

Figure 8 *Tutankhamun wearing the crown of Upper Egypt. Luxor Temple. Photograph courtesy of Dave Thompson.*

The *Khepresh* or blue crown, commonly believed to represent the war crown
The *Ibes* crown
The double plumes of Amun
A number of linen wig-covers

None of these crowns, other than the linen wig covers, have been discovered and it is uncertain what they were made of. It is likely that the crowns used for the coronation ceremony were kept in the temple stores and used for all kings. During the crowning ceremony, Tutankhamun was presented with the crook and flail; a small, child-sized set was discovered in his tomb and are likely to be those given to him at this ceremony (Plate 8). There is also a larger set, bearing his later name of Tutankhamun, rather than Tutankhaten and inscribed: 'The good god, the beloved. Glittering in his face like Aten when he rises, son of Amun'; indicating that, as the new king grew, a new crook and flail were made for him. These were the sign of his royal status and he would rarely have been seen in state without them in his hands.

The next sign of Tutankhamun's kingship was when he was presented with the five-fold titulary that confirmed his new royal status. These titles were very important:

'The Horus (*Hr*) Name' associating the king with the god Horus

'He of the two ladies' (*Nebti*)' The two ladies in this title represent the vulture goddess, Nekhbet, from El Kab in Upper Egypt and the cobra goddess, Wadjet, from Buto in Lower Egypt, showing his role as king of Upper and Lower Egypt.

'The Golden Horus' (*Hr nwb*) name is not fully understood. It has been suggested that the title reflects the Egyptian king's control over the region of the gold mines in Nubia.

'The Throne name', was given to the king when he became king and was followed by the *nsw bity* (He of the sedge and the bee), showing the king as ruler of Upper and Lower Egypt. The Throne name of Tutankhaten was Nebkheprure and was the name by which Egyptians identified him.

'The birth name' followed by the *sa ra* (Son of Ra), showing the divinity of the king. These last two names were written within a cartouche.

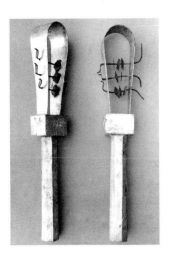

Plate 1 *Two sistra which would have belonged to female members of Tutankhamun's family. Copyright Griffith Institute, Oxford.*

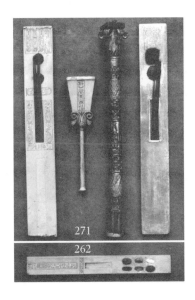

Plate 2 *Meritaten's palette (number 262) and the papyrus burnisher (271). Copyright Griffith Institute, Oxford.*

Plate 3 *Fly whisks of horse hair. Copyright Griffith Institute, Oxford.*

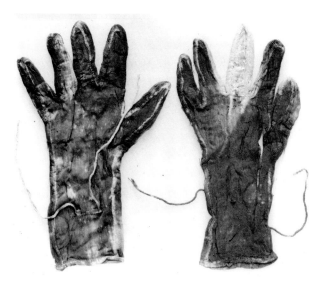

Plate 4 *Child-sized linen gloves. Copyright Griffith Institute, Oxford.*

Plate 5 *Riding gauntlet. Copyright Griffith Institute, Oxford.*

Plate 6 *Ankhesenamun hands Tutankhamun an arrow. Copyright Griffith Institute, Oxford.*

Plate 7 *Two of Tutankhamun's four senet sets. Copyright Griffith Institute, Oxford.*

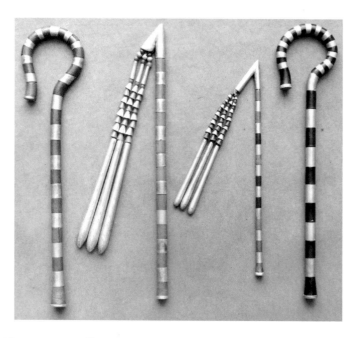

Plate 8 *Two sets of 'crook and flail'. One set is smaller than the other and would have been used when he was a child. Copyright Griffith Institute, Oxford.*

Plate 9 *Lid of ivory box showing Tutankhamun and Ankhesenamun in the garden. Copyright Griffith Institute, Oxford.*

Plate 10 *One of the many wine jars with the hieratic label. Copyright Griffith Institute, Oxford.*

Plate 11 *A matching throne and footstool which would have stood in Tutankhamun's palace. Copyright Griffith Institute, Oxford.*

Plate 12 *Foreign shoe. Probably a diplomatic gift. Copyright Griffith Institute, Oxford.*

Plate 13 *Folding portable chairs. Copyright Griffith Institute, Oxford.*

Plate 14 *Decorated tunic worn by Tutankhamun. Copyright Griffith Institute, Oxford.*

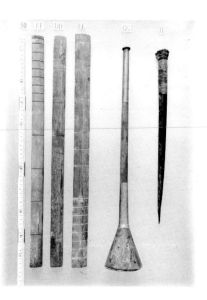

Plate 15 *Measuring sticks and trumpet from the tomb. Copyright Griffith Institute, Oxford.*

Plate 16 *Preserved head of Tutankhamun. Copyright Griffith Institute, Oxford.*

Once Tutankhamun Nebkheperure had been given his royal titles he was accepted as the new king and was entitled to carry out the rituals to the statue of Amun in the sanctuary at Karnak for the first time as king.[1] These rituals involved cleaning and dressing the statue and making offerings of food, water, beer, linen and flowers, all accompanied by prayers and incantations. Tutankhamun would have needed to train for this part of the coronation ceremony as it was important to recite the prayers and perform the rituals accurately. This would have been a daunting task for an adult prince but was particularly terrifying for a small child of nine years old, even if he had been raised to expect to be king.

After this final part of the ceremony had ended, Tutankhamun would have left the temple wearing one of the crowns and the ceremonial bull's tail, clutching his crook and flail, all representing his new status as king to the waiting crowds. He also wore a set of ceremonial jewellery. Adorned in his new regalia, he participated in a huge public procession, allowing the population to see their new king and know that *maat* (cosmic balance) was restored. This procession of dancers, musicians and military personnel was accompanied by many days of feasting and drinking. A public holiday was declared, so the entire population could participate in celebrating the ascent of the new king.

Once on the throne, Tutankhamun married Ankhesenepaten, his half-sister (Figure 9) who had previously been married to her father, Akhenaten and then to Smenkhkare. When Tutankhaten changed his name to Tutankhamun she changed hers to Ankhesenamun, to show the renewed worship of the traditional gods (Figures 10 and 11). Ankhesenamun was possibly a couple of years older than Tutankhamun and it is likely that they grew up together at Akhetaten. Their close relationship is reflected in the images of them together, which show a great deal of intimacy and affection. This is considered by some as a sign of their love for each other and perhaps it was, although it needs to be remembered that

Figure 9 *Tutankhamun and Ankhesenamun. Luxor temple. Photograph courtesy of Dave Thompson.*

although Amarna art is more naturalistic, it is still stylistic and may not reflect their true feelings.

Tutankhamun and Ankhesenamun had no surviving children, meaning there was no clear heir to the throne. However, it seems they had some offspring; the bodies of two female babies were buried in his tomb. They were found in two small anthropoid coffins placed within a plain white box, side by side and head to foot. The coffins were not designed as a set; the feet of one of the anthropoid coffins were sawn off so the lid of the chest could be closed. Neither of the girls was named. On their coffins, they are simply referred to as 'Osiris', in reference to their deceased and reborn status. It is possible that these children died so young they had not participated in a naming ceremony and hence had not been fully acknowledged as royal children. It is thought that names were given at a certain age, although exactly what age is not known. Many infants died in the first few weeks of life, before a

Figure 10 *Tutankhamun as Amun. Karnak Temple. Photograph courtesy of Dave Thompson.*

name could be given. Both bodies were mummified traditionally and the smaller of the two wore a gilded cartonnage (linen covered in plaster) mask several sizes too big for her; clearly not made for her. The larger of the girls did not have a mask; it could be suggested that there was only one child's mask in storage at the time and neither time (nor inclination) to provide her with one of her own. The smaller girl was very premature; it is likely that she was still-born, as she was in the fifth month of gestation. 21 mm of the umbilical cord was still attached and she was just over 25 cm in length.[2] Her organs were not removed for mummification and she had no jewellery or amulets amidst the wrappings. The larger girl was approximately 36 cm in length and was in the seventh month

Figure 11 *Ankhesenamun as Amunet. Karnak Temple. Photograph courtesy of Dave Thompson.*

of gestation. Her skull had been damaged since discovery but she had no umbilical cord, indicating she may have survived birth but died very shortly after, due to her prematurity (although Harrison noted that her facial features indicate that she was still-born in the later months of gestation).[3] She was traditionally mummified; her brain had been removed through the nose and her internal organs removed through a slit in the left hand side of her abdomen. Her head and chest were packed with linen packages filled with natron to preserve the shape of her body and to continue the drying process. She also did not possess any jewellery or amulets within her bandages. X-rays indicate this child suffered from Sprengel's deformity in her left shoulder. This affects the shoulder, pushing the shoulder blade upwards. She also suffered from spina bifida and scoliosis (curvature of the spine) so would have had an extremely difficult life had she survived.

In 1971, the Cairo Museum gave permission for the bodies to be re-examined but when the coffins were opened the bodies were not inside. Derry, who originally studied the bodies, had not returned them. The larger girl was found in the Cairo Musuem stores but the smaller girl was not discovered until 1992 in the Kasr el Einy Hospital, together with 526 other mummies Derry had neglected to return.[4] On the discovery of the larger girl, Harrison tried to identify her parents through the study of blood groups but this was sadly inconclusive; she could have been the child of Thutmosis III, Yuya and Thuya, Tutankhamun or Smenkhkare.[5] Until DNA testing can be carried out on the known mummies from this period we will have to be content with knowing she is of the Thutmosid family. DNA testing, in its current state of development, is often inconclusive and causes damage to the mummies. The Egyptian government will not allow this testing to be carried out on the mummies in Egypt.

It has been suggested that the bodies, rather than being Tutankhamun's children, stored after their death to await the burial of their father, were not his children but bodies placed in the tomb enabling him to have children in the afterlife, although where these children came from is not specified.[6] Also, if this is the case, then surely full-term babies would have been used rather than those who did not survive birth. There is circumstantial evidence to suggest that Tutankhamun had other children, whose names and bodies are now inaccessible to us. The first piece of evidence comes from a letter in the Amarna archive from the Babylonian king Burnaburiash, perhaps written to Tutankhamun. The greetings at the head of the letter, although formal, show a certain amount of intimacy between the two rulers. The Babylonian addresses Tutankhamun: 'All hail to you, your house, your wives, your children, your country, your nobles, your horses and your chariots'.[7] The reference to his 'children' would have been a major diplomatic blunder if Tutankhamun were childless and would not have benefited the king in his requests of diplomatic gifts from Tutankhamun. The Babylonian king also mentions 'wives', indicating that Tutankhamun had more than one. Although we only know of Ankhesenamun as his wife, it was unusual for the Egyptian king to only have one wife; he may even have inherited a harem on his ascent to the throne. Taemwadjsi, sister of the newly appointed Viceroy of Nubia Huy, held the title of 'Matron of the Harem of Tutankhamun' indicating that there was a harem housing the wives of the king. It has been suggested that as Taemwadjsi spent much time in Nubia she was filling the harem with elite, Nubian women, of a calibre suitable for the king.[8] The second piece of circumstantial evidence indicating that Tutankhamun had surviving children is found on an ivory chest (JE 61477) in the tomb, which shows him and Ankhesenamun relaxing in a garden, as their children play nearby (Plate 9). It would be unusual for dead children to be depicted and the image is unlikely to represent the two babies from the tomb, as they died before they had a chance for life. However, it is possible that these images of children are smaller images of Tutankhamun and his wife.

Although circumstantial, these pieces of evidence could suggest that there were another two children of Tutankhamun, who were the legitimate heirs to the throne, unless they, like the still-born children, were girls. If they were boys, that raises the question of what happened to them. Did they die young? Were they buried in their own tombs in the Valley of the Kings? Did they die of natural causes or does this add another level of intrigue to the story of Tutankhamun?

Tutankhamun's first major act of his reign was to change his name from Tutankhaten to Tutankhamun to show his new-found loyalty to Amun. For the first couple of years of his reign, Tutankhamun and Ankhesenamun remained in Amarna, possibly at the North Palace, their childhood home. Then, the capital city was moved from Akhetaten to the traditional administrative capital of Memphis, in year two or three (1332–1331 BCE) of his reign. Initially the royal court was moved to Memphis, where the coronation of Tutankhamun took place, but the focus of his building works at Thebes indicate that he also resided here for part of his reign, probably at the palace of his grandfather, Amenhotep III, in Malkata.

The remains of the palace at Malkata are now only identified by very scanty mud-brick foundations but it was a beautifully decorated palace (Figure 12), with pleasure gardens and a pool. Images

Figure 12 *Decoration at Malkata. Photograph courtesy of Wayne Frostick.*

on the ivory casket (JE16477) within his tomb depict some of the pleasure gardens that may have adorned Malkata, or indeed any of the palaces he inhabited during his reign. On this casket, Tutankhamun and his wife Ankhesenamun stand beneath a pergola entwined with grape vines. She is clutching two bouquets of papyrus, poppies and lotus flowers which she offers to her husband. The garden is filled with cornflowers, mandrakes and poppies, the latter two being gathered by their two children (or themselves, depending on the interpretation of the image). The garden had a small fish pond to add to its beauty, which attracted birds and the palace cats; shade was provided by pergolas and trees. It is likely that Tutankhamun and Ankhesenamun spent many hours sitting in or walking through these gardens, watching the birds and fish and breathing in the beautiful scents of the flowers and trees.[9] There are further scenes of the young couple in a garden on the small golden shrine in his tomb, which shows Ankhesenamun bringing flowers to Tutankhamun and tying a floral necklace around his neck. He responds by adorning her hands with perfumed oil; snapshots of the private life of Tutankhamun and his wife. These scenes show great intimacy between the king and queen and it is possible to interpret these scenes as happy interludes in the otherwise turbulent life of these two children. Ankhesenamun, at this point, was married to her third husband; perhaps she was content with a husband of similar age, with whom she had grown up. Before politics of kingship took him away, they probably spent much of their days in frivolous activities and it would be lovely to think that, throughout his reign, when time permitted, they snatched private moments together.

However, Amarna art focuses heavily on images of nature and these images of Tutankhamun and Ankhesenamun passing the time in the garden may not reflect their real lives but rather the artistic style of the period. The same can be said for the very intimate scenes of the royal couple, which could reflect their intimate feelings for each other or could be another form of Amarna artistic style. Any Egyptian art has to be interpreted very carefully; all periods use very distinctive characteristics to get information across to the viewer. As a small boy, the flowers in the gardens may not have interested Tutankhamun a great deal but he no doubt understood the importance of the lotus and papyrus as symbols of Upper and Lower Egypt and was familiar with their forms, as they were used on furniture, wall decoration, clothes and shoes which he saw every day.

Travelling between the two new capitals of Thebes and Memphis, the king would pass through much agricultural land; due to his inquisitive nature, Tutankhamun may have learned about the plants and made connections between them and the food that ended up on his plate at meal times. From the study of the cereals discovered in the tomb of Tutankhamun, one scholar has tried to reconstruct the environment in which he lived. By studying the weeds and inclusions in the barley found there, these fields Tutankhamun knew have been reconstructed virtually. The reconstruction of the landscape showed it greatly resembled modern Egypt, although the amount of agricultural land on either side of the Nile was narrower. The scholar reconstructed an average barley field in March and April, showing it included a number of weeds, including wild sorghum, black cumin (which flowers with delicate white and purple flowers), slender foxtail, wild mullet, donnel and water plantain (which also has delicate white flowers).[10] Some of the plants stood taller than the barley and would have been visible from the road. It may have been part of Tutankhamun's royal education as king to travel the fields with the vizier when taxes were being collected, so that he could relate the cereals to the taxes collected and learn their relative value.

As a child, visiting his grandfather at the palace of Malkata, Tutankhamun may have learned much about horticulture. In the palace library were books called 'The Book of the *Moringa* tree' and

'The Book of the Pomegranate Tree', the contents of which are now lost but they were clearly horticultural tomes.[11] He also had the pleasure of playing on Queen Tiye's lake. This lake was enormous, 1.6 km long by 0.4 km wide; the current archaeological remains are dominated by the mounds of soil excavated from this lake. Tiye owned a boat, *The Aten shines*, which she may have sailed on the lake – a pleasant way for a grandmother to entertain her young grandson. Potentially, these were visits relished by the young prince as a little adventure, outside the religious and somewhat intense city of his father. It must have been a strange experience for Tutankhamun to live in Malkata as king, walking along corridors filled with the ghosts of his dead family.

Although the royal family and the palace administration left the city of Akhetaten in year three or four (1331–1330 BCE), it was not completely abandoned and remained inhabited until the reign of Horemheb (1321 BCE), albeit with a fraction of the population. As the temples and workshops shut down, there was little left to encourage the elite of the city to remain, so they returned to their own villages and cities throughout Egypt. Only the working classes remained in Amarna, in the still-functioning faience factories.

Not long after Amarna was abandoned as the capital, Tutankhamun reburied the person in tomb KV55, known as the 'Amarna cache', in the Valley of the Kings. This body is widely believed to be that of his brother, Smenkhkare (see Chapter 3). When discovered, this tomb was believed to be the burial place of Tutankhamun, as the door was sealed with his royal seal (Figure 13). Once inside, the archaeologists put together a completely different scenario. Although Smenkhkare died at Akhetaten and was given a royal funeral there, Tutankhamun reburied him at Thebes. The reburial was accompanied by a traditional funeral and it is possible that the young King Tutankhamun resided over it, wearing a leopardskin cloak, in the role of *sem* priest.

Figure 13 *Seal from Tutankhamun's tomb door, the same as the one used to seal Smenkhkare's tomb. Ashmolean Museum. Photograph courtesy of Wayne Frostick.*

Smenkhkare's royal burial at Amarna was accompanied by a number of gold funerary goods to facilitate his rebirth into the afterlife. However, when he was reburied these royal burial goods were removed and replaced by others from the Theban stores. The goods that originally belonged to Smenkhkare were re-used by Tutankhamun in his own burial, suggesting that they were stored for his future use.

One of the strangest aspects of the KV55 excavations was the discovery of the dismantled gilded wooden shrine of Queen Tiye, which had been left in the entrance corridor. The archaeologists placed a number of wooden planks over it, so visitors could enter the tomb, which irreparably damaged the shrine. A visiting tourist, Charles Connolly, reported in his diary that 'gold leaf seemed to be flying through the air in every direction' and another tourist was invited to 'collect handfuls of the gold-filled dust'.[12] Who can be sure what secrets this shrine may have uncovered if it had been conserved and removed from the tomb?

As there were a number of Tiye's other funerary goods in KV55 it is thought that Tutankhamun may have rescued them from her

Amarnan tomb at the same time as Smenkhkare was re-buried. He may have located her Amarnan tomb and removed her funerary goods in an attempt to preserve her memory from possible religious retribution against the Aten cult. She was probably originally buried in a tomb constructed by her husband Amenhotep III, perhaps even in his tomb in the Valley of the Kings. Although Amenhotep III was safe from the political destruction of the Amarna retribution, Tiye, as a resident of the new city was in danger. Tutankhamun probably could not bear the thought of the body of his beloved grandmother being desecrated. It was clear that Tutankhamun was close to his grandmother; a lock of her red-gold hair was found in his tomb. The body now thought to be hers, the so-called 'Elder Lady', was located in KV35, the tomb of Amenhotep II. The mummy of the 'Younger Lady', also found in this tomb, has recently been the focus of a theory that it may be that of the enigmatic Nefertiti.[13] However, a recent chromosome test suggests that the body is probably that of an as-yet unidentified young man rather than a young woman.[14]

At the time of its discovery, the KV55 body was sent by Arthur Weigall to be examined by Elliot-Smith. It was already in skeletal form; upon opening the tomb the soft tissues disintegrated. Elliot-Smith was expecting the body of an elderly woman, the dowager Queen Tiye and was rather surprised to receive the bones of a young man. The questions regarding the body in KV55 have yet to be answered to the satisfaction of all scholars, although it is generally accepted that the body is Smenkhkare, a man who died in his early twenties.

Tutankhamun was brought up in Akhetaten and had no knowledge of any other religion than the Aten cult, yet his reign was dominated by the re-establishment of the traditional religion, one totally alien to him. It is clear some very influential advisors guided him in his royal decrees. One of the most important advisors was Horemheb, general of the army throughout the reign

of Akhenaten, Tutankhamun and even Ay. He was given
the title of 'Deputy King' under Tutankhamun and was very
important in the royal administration. On a statue of Horemheb
and his wife Mutnodjmet (currently in Turin), it is recorded that
he was often called to calm down the king when he 'had fallen into
a rage', indicating his influence over the young child:

> The heart of the king was pleased with his work, agreeing with
> his decisions. He made him Lord of the land in order to main-
> tain the law of the land as Hereditary Prince. He was unique
> without equal. All the plans for the Two Lands came from his
> hands. Everyone agreed with what he said when he was sum-
> moned by the king. Now the palace fell into a rage and he
> answered back to the king.[15]

It is clear that Horemheb had a positive influence over the young
king, but also that he needed to swallow his pride when dealing
with a small child's temper. He seems to have a great deal of power,
not only over the king as 'all the plans ... came from his hands', but
also over the rest of the court as 'everyone agreed with him', which
shows him to have been an influential, charming and diplomatic
man with an incredible intellect that people greatly admired.
However, many scholars interpret this as proof that he was a military bully, full of ambition but without scruples. This seems
unlikely, as he was able to maintain the trust of three kings
(Akhenaten, Tutankhamun and Ay) of very different natures and
to continue to rise in power and influence until he became Deputy
King. If he were the ambitious bully that he is often depicted as,
surely someone would have seen through the façade?

Another influential official was Ay, the Vizier. This was the most
important administrator in Egypt, privy to all the king's business
and responsible for the control of all traffic in and out of the palace,
including messengers to all parts of the Egyptian empire. He was
responsible for passing reports regarding the entire kingdom to the

king and therefore had a great deal of power and influence. He was also Tutankhamun's great uncle, brother of Queen Tiye and possibly the father of Nefertiti. The third important official was Maya, 'Overseer of the Treasury'. He held this title under Tutankhamun, Ay and Horemheb and it is likely that he was also in Amarna, albeit in a lower administrative position, which enabled him to become close to the royal family. Maya held his high position for nearly twenty years, dying in year nine of Horemheb's reign.

Although the young king was involved in the politics of the day (which will be discussed in Chapter 5), there was still plenty of time for him to participate in and enjoy the luxury of palace life. The palace of Malkata, a place of great extravagance, was his royal residence for a short while. Malkata was not just a palace but an enormous, self-sufficient city, covering over three square kilometres. It included buildings, temples, villas, parade grounds, faience factories and workshops. The palace complex was immense and it housed the large pleasure lake of Queen Tiye, Tutankhamun's grandmother. From the excavations, it is possible to see there were three building stages at the palace, as there were three levels of floor, each with new plaster and a fresh design. At least one of these stages may have been added by the young king.

This palace was one-storey, with windows high up in the walls providing light and a cooling breeze. Some of the rooms may have been open to the sky, allowing the king to watch the flight of the hawks. Large faience hieroglyphic inlays decorated the outside of the palace, which was painted white. Many of the internal walls were decorated with geometric patterns or naturalistic scenes of plants, trees or animals, rather similar to those at Amarna. Although completed by Amenhotep III, these images probably reminded Tutankhamun of his childhood. The palace contained a number of audience chambers, each dominated by a throne. The pavement leading to the throne dais bore designs of captive

Asiatics, Nubians and bows, so that the king trampled these ene-
mies as he walked to his throne. The throne had a mud-brick core,
covered with a bright yellow painted limestone casing, incised with
blue and red hieroglyphs. The rooms of the palace had elaborately
decorated painted pavements, including one showing a marsh
scene complete with swimming ducks, fish and geese. The royal
bedchamber had the thickest walls in the palace, to protect the
young king while he was asleep and at his most vulnerable. Its walls
were decorated with the *sa* and the *ankh*, signs of protection and
with images of Bes, the dwarf god of fertility, childbirth and frivo-
lity. Sadly, this deity's influence did not help the young king in the
production of a living heir. There was a large banqueting hall over
thirty metres long, its ceiling supported by eighteen wooden
columns with stone bases. The end of the room where the king and
queen sat was elaborately decorated with images of the king on his
throne, whereas the other end of the hall was much plainer. This
banqueting hall doubtless saw some great feasts, with streams of
servants bringing tray after tray of elaborate rich food and guests
entertained by dancing girls and musicians of the type displayed in
New Kingdom non-royal tombs.

Although the food in the tomb of Tutankhamun was designed
for his afterlife and the maintenance of the cult of the *ka*, it could be
presumed that the food placed in the tomb included the young
king's favourites – could there be anything worse than having to
eat, for eternity, food not to your taste? Such food may have
appeared at a number of the feasts at the palace of Malkata. It
would be nice to think that the royal cook was consulted when
putting together the funerary menu. Tutankhamun's *ka* was well
catered for, with a number of boxes of food placed in the tomb.
However, the labelling on the boxes was careless; only forty per
cent of the labels match the contents.[16] It would seem that the
boxes were labelled in advance and the cuts of meat were substi-
tuted at the last minute. There can be no doubt that Tutankhamun

enjoyed meat; the funerary food was dominated by cuts of oxen and geese, accompanied by numerous baskets of plants and seeds. Some of the cuts of meat are not to modern western taste but were considered prime cuts to the ancient Egyptians. Indeed, the entire animal was used in the royal kitchen, including the head, ribs and rump.[17] No doubt the meat was accompanied by various sauces and vegetables, although what these were can only be guessed from the plant materials in the tomb. The sauces may have included coriander, chickpeas and lentils. Fruit featured heavily in the diet of the king and in the diet of ordinary people, including sycamore figs, dom-palm fruit and dates. (Dom palm fruit tastes of ginger and was used for flavouring food.)

The staples of the Egyptian diet were bread and beer. In the tomb the raw ingredients were there: barley for beer making and emmer wheat for bread making.[18] There were also over a dozen loaves of bread. These loaves were semi-circular, up to 13 × 7 cm in size and all but one contained berries from the Christ-thorn plant and could be classified as cakes or fruit loaves.[19] Coriander, garlic, juniper berries, black cumin, wild thyme, fenugreek seeds and pepper may have been used to season Tutankhamun's food.[20] Coriander was imported from Palestine, Syria, or Iraq and was rare and expensive but nonetheless was in the tomb. Chickpeas and lentils, native to Egypt, may have formed the basis of a dip or soup and were a basic staple of Tutankhamun's (and everyone else's) daily diet. Playing *senet* with his wife, or sitting in the evening talking with friends, Tutankhamun would have snacked on almonds, raisins and watermelon seeds. The tomb also contained a jar labelled 'honey of good quality', indicating that honey featured in the king's desserts.[21] Honey cakes were popular in ancient Egypt and were one of the few things that satisfied a sweet tooth.

The ingredients for making beer were also provided in the tomb but the finished product was not included. However, Tutankhamun would have been able to instruct his *shabtis* (servant statues) to produce this staple for him in the afterlife. Hundreds of these servants were placed in the tomb of Tutankhamun, charged with the obligation of working for the king in the afterlife on any task that he might be asked to carry out. *Shabtis* were not just for the king; by the eighteenth dynasty both royal and non-royal burials included a large number. Blocks for grinding the barley and wheat were provided to help the beer-making process. In addition to the staple beer there were twenty-six amphorae jars (tall clay vessels with pointed bottoms) of wine in the tomb of Tutankhamun, indicating that he was fond of a goblet of wine with his food. The wine has completely evaporated, leaving nothing but a few traces at the bottom of the jars, which were recently analysed by a team from Barcelona.[22] On each of the amphorae were hieratic labels giving the date of the wine, the vineyard and the vintner (Plate 10):

Year 4. Sweet wine of the House of Aten, Life Prosperity Health! of the Western River. Chief Vintner Aperershop

Year 4. Sweet wine of the House of Aten, Life Prosperity Health! of the Western River. Chief Vintner Nen.

Year 4. Shedeh of very good quality of the House of Aten, Life Prosperity Health! of the Western River. Chief Vintner Nen.

Year 4. Wine of the House of Tutankhamun, Life Prosperity Health! in the Western River, from the Chief Vintner Kha'y.

Year 4. Shedeh of very good quality of the House of Aten, of the Western River. Chief Vintner Kha'y

Year 5. Wine of the House of Aten of the Western River. Chief Vintner Any.

Year 5. Wine of the House of Aten of the Western River. Chief Vintner Pinehas.

Year 5.   Sweet wine of the House of Aten from Tjel. Chief Vintner Penamun.

Year 5.   Wine of the House of Aten of the Western River. Chief Vintner Nenia.

Year 5.   Sweet wine of the House of Aten of the Western River. Chief Vintner Nakht.

Year 5.   Sweet wine of the House of Aten of the Western River. From the Chief Vintner Nakhtsobek.

Year 5.   Sweet wine of the House of Aten from Karet. Chief Vintner Ramose.

Year 5.   Shedeh of very good quality of the House of Aten, of the Western River. Chief Vintner Rer.

Year 5.   Wine of the House of Tutankhamun, Ruler of the Southern Heliopolis, in the Western River, from the Chief Vintner Kha'y.

Year 5.   Wine of the House of Tutankhamun, Life Prosperity Health, in the Western River, from the Chief Vintner Kha'y.

Year 5.   Wine of the House of Tutankhamun, Ruler of the Southern Heliopolis, L.P.H. in the Western River, from the Chief Vintner Kha'y.

Year 5.   Wine of the House of Tutankhamun, Ruler of the Southern Heliopolis, L.P.H. in the Western River, from the Chief Vintner Kha'y.

Year 9.   Wine of the house of Aten on the Western River. By the Chief Vintner Pay.

Year 9.   Wine of the House of Tutankhamun, Ruler of the Southern Heliopolis, L.P.H. in the Western River, from the Chief Vintner May.

Year 9.   Wine of the house of Aten on the Western River. Chief Vintner Nebnufe

Year 9.   Wine of the house of Aten in the Western River. By the Chief Vintner Nakhtsobek.

Year 9.   Wine of the House of Aten of the Western River. Chief Vintner Sennufe.

Year 9.   Wine of the House of Tutankhamun, Ruler of the Southern Heliopolis, L.P.H. Sennufe.

Year *10.*   Wine of good quality from Iaty

Year 31.   Wine of the House ... Vizier Penthu[23]

Four main vineyards functioned during the reign of Tutankhamun: The House of the Aten on the Western River, The House of Tutankhamun, Ruler of Southern Heliopolis, House of Aten from Tjel and House of Aten from Karet. When Tutankhamun opened his own vineyard, he probably visited to see wine-making in progress. The wine from this vineyard is dated to year 5 (1329 BCE) of his reign, when Tutankhamun was only thirteen or fourteen years old. On his first visit to the vineyard he probably met the vintners Kha'y and May and perhaps on subsequent visits he met Sennufe, who probably indulged the young king by taking him on a tour of the vineyard and processing area. The location of this vineyard is not known, although some eighteenth dynasty vineyards were located in the Delta, where the land is particularly fertile. From the Old Kingdom (2686 BCE) onwards vineyards were often protected from the desert *khamsin* winds by a high enclosure wall and this may also have been the case during the New Kingdom (1540 BCE on). Many Theban noble's tombs from the eighteenth dynasty depict wine-making, indicating that Thebes was a particularly good area for growing grapes and producing wine. Many different colours and taste of grapes grew in Egypt at the time and the vintners may have explained these differences to the king. Malkata wine labels include the word 'blended', indicating that different grapes were mixed to produce different flavours and each vineyard had its own special blend of wine. As with vineyard tours in the modern world, the king was probably actively encouraged to taste the different varieties of wine and savour their flavours.

The process of wine making was probably demonstrated and the thirteen year old king may have asked if he could join in. The process started with the picking of the grapes, which required knowledge of ripeness and suitability. The baskets of grapes were emptied into vats made of clay, wood or stone. Unfortunately, no examples have survived into the archaeological record, although the tomb images depicting vineyards show they were used. The clay vats were plastered with gypsum to make them watertight and to compensate for the low acidity in the grapes. Then the grapes were crushed by foot. Four to six men climbed into the vat, held on to straps hanging from a frame above them and trod on the grapes until they were liquid. To counteract the monotony of the job and to maintain rhythm, an additional employee would play the clappers or other musical instruments.[24] For a royal visit, the musicians hired to keep time were probably the best; a spectacle worthy of royalty. The vintners would explain that the colour of wines varied and to produce white wine the red grape skins needed to be removed. Middle Kingdom (from 1900 BCE) tomb scenes from Meir show greenish-brown grapes, indicating that they could produce white wine, which may have been available in the wine cellar of an eighteenth dynasty king.[25] At Malkata, the hieratic labels on the wine amphorae show that there were various reasons why wine was manufactured and indicate the quality of wine depended on the use it was put to. There was 'wine for offerings', 'wine for taxes', 'wine for a happy return' and 'wine for merry-making'. The grape mulch from the vats was placed into a large sheet of linen tied between two poles. The poles were twisted, both clockwise, to squeeze out the liquid, which was collected in pottery vessels. This process required great strength; in the tomb scenes there are sometimes five people involved in the twisting of one cloth. The juice in the pottery jars was left to ferment before being transferred to racked jars, stoppered with perforated seals to allow the carbon monoxide to escape.[26] After fermentation was complete, the wine was ready to drink.

Figure 14 *Wine strainer. Louvre Museum. Photograph courtesy of Wayne Frostick.*

Tutankhamun clearly enjoyed drinking wine, as the twenty-six jars in his tomb suggest. There was also a wine strainer (Figure 14), which prevented dregs from getting into his wine goblet and spoiling the flavour of the wine, perhaps indicating he was a connoisseur. Although for the ordinary people wine was something of a luxury, for the royal household it was a tasty but expensive alternative to beer. Athenaeus, writing in 200 CE described Egyptian wines as 'pale, pleasant, aromatic and mildly astringent, with an oily quality dissolved with water'. Although this may have been an accurate description of the wine, whereas the Greeks watered their wine down, the Egyptians did not, indicating that the oily texture was palatable to the average Egyptian wine connoisseur.[27] The consumption of wine by the upper elite and royalty meant the production of wine amphorae was expensive and there is evidence that the ancient Egyptians recycled their wine jars.[28]

Two amphorae of another beverage, *shedeh*, were also placed in the tomb. *Shedeh* was a popular drink in the New Kingdom and interests scholars. The Egyptian texts give very little information about its ingredients but an ancient school text declares 'if only you knew that wine is an abomination you would abjure *shedeh* drink, you would not set the beer jar in your heart, you would forget *thrk* -wine', making it clear, as it is listed with other alcoholic beverages, that *shedeh* was alcoholic.[29] Papyrus Salt states that *shedeh* was a gift from the sun god Ra to his sons, making it a divine and therefore a luxury tipple, although during the Ramesside and Ptolemaic Periods it was included in the temple offering lists. New Kingdom love poetry associates *shedeh* with the voice of a lover, giving it aphrodisiacal properties. All this indicates that *shedeh* was considered to be a luxurious and desirable drink; perfect refreshment for the king. It seems that despite its desirability it was quite rare; of the hundreds of labelled amphorae from Deir el Medina, Malkata and Amarna, only fifteen record *shedeh*, including Maya's Memphite tomb and the tomb of Tutankhamun, suggesting that it was more popular during this period.[30] However, as there were only two jars of *shedeh* in the twenty-six amphorae in his tomb, this indicates its rarity.

It is commonly believed that *shedeh* was made from pomegranates, rather than grapes.[31] Further studies have suggested that it may have been a heated wine, made using traditional methods. Papyrus Salt 825 (715–332 BCE) describes the method; sadly the ingredients are missing: 'It is ... repeat the filtration: heating again. This is the way to prepare the *Shedeh*'. The team from Barcelona investigated this missing information by using liquid chromatography and mass spectrometry to determine the exact chemical composition of the substance removed from the bottom of the jar.[32] The presence of tartaric acid within the sample jar of *shedeh* shows it was made of grapes, as those grown in the Mediterranean and Near East exclusively contain this type of acid. Syringic acid, a marker of red wine, was also discovered in the sample. These acids indicate that *shedeh* was made from red grapes and not pomegranates.[33] Heating the *shedeh* may have given it the flavour of mulled wine and made *shedeh* different from the traditional wine of Egypt, and a favourite luxury of the king.

The examination of Tutankhamun's body showed he had pierced ears; although no earrings were found on his body, a number were discovered in his tomb. The holes in his ears were larger than modern piercings at 7.5 mm wide. The mummy also showed evidence of very long eyelashes, of the sort that could render him very desirable to the opposite sex. The mummy had a totally shaved head. This was not unusual for ancient Egyptians: most shaved their hair as a defence against head lice – something from which not even royalty was immune. Tutankhamun had started to shave, as would be expected of an eighteen year old; boxes containing his cosmetic items were discovered in the tomb. A label on an ivory box lists the items that were originally placed within (although they had been taken by robbers): 'The bag of his Majesty, Life Prosperity Health, when he was a child ... What is therein; copper, razors ... alabaster ewers'.[34] These ewers were containers used in the shaving process. The word 'bag' does not apply to the ivory box; perhaps a bag was placed within the box and held the objects.[35] When he was a child, the shaving equipment would perhaps have been used for shaving his head; as he got older, he would have started to shave his face. When the mummy was examined, no pubic hair was visible. Like many Egyptians, he may have removed all his body hair as a means of keeping clean, or possibly the hair loss may have been due to the mummification process. Lice were rife in ancient Egypt and did not discriminate between rich and poor; cleanliness was paramount in everyone's daily routine and shaving was a major part of it.[36]

It is often a surprise to modern readers to discover that ancient Egyptian men wore just as much make-up and perfume as women and adorned their bodies with oils and unguents to prevent dry skin and to improve the way they smelled. The richer the individual, the more numerous were his unguents. King Tutankhamun had a large collection – thirty-five calcite jars in the annexe of his tomb stored more than 350 litres of perfume and oils. Unfortunately, due to their high market value, the tomb robbers who entered the tomb shortly after his burial emptied these jars of their contents, even scraping out the bottom so as not to leave any behind. Luckily, a small amount was left in one of the jars, which was analysed by Kew Gardens and the British Museum. It proved to be ninety per cent animal fat and ten per cent resin or balm, though its particular use is unknown.[37] The contents of the other jars remains unknown, although records from other sources give information on the oils that were available during his reign and therefore what he may have used. These aromatic oils may have included balanos oil, safflower oil, linseed oil, *ben* oil (moringa), olive oil, almond oil, sesame oil and other perfume oils made from fragrant resins and bark. Perfume making and the materials used are listed and depicted in many tombs, although what was placed in the tomb can only be guessed at. Lumps of frankincense, which had a variety of uses, including as a deodorant, an unguent for anointing the body and for burning as incense, were discovered in the tomb. An hieratic label accompanied these lumps of incense: 'The bag of His majesty Life Prosperity Health when he was a boy ... what is in it; incense and gum'.[38] Whether these lumps were those he had owned as a child or were new at the time of burial we will never know; but these three thousand year old lumps of frankincense smelled strongly when they were discovered, no doubt a fraction of the original aroma.

It is quite clear that as young prince and later king, Tutankhamun wore eye-paint, as was traditional for both men and women. In the tomb, the lid of a box was discovered, unfortunately separated from the rest of the box, which bore the hieratic inscription: 'The bag of pharaoh Life Prosperity and Health when he was a boy ... Gold; 1 basket 1 jar (earthenware pot) of water ... a stick for applying eye-paint ... 3 grasshoppers of gold'. The container eventually matched to the lid was empty; its contents had clearly been removed by the tomb robbers.[39] Although the basket of gold and the pot of water are interesting, the three golden grasshoppers and the stick for applying eye paint are more relevant. 'Grasshoppers' probably refers to cosmetic containers in the shape of grasshoppers, the wings of which unfolded to reveal the dish beneath. (Howard Carter is said secretly to have taken one of these from the tomb during the excavations.) The stick for applying eye-paint was a kohl stick, the likes of which have been found in their hundreds from ancient Egypt. The label states that these objects belonged to Tutankhamun when he was a child, showing he would have learned how to apply eye make-up when young. These early practice runs were doubtless quite eye-catching and probably involved a lot of make-up remover and kohl in the eye. After he had learned to apply the eye-paint accurately he probably became quick and perhaps even experimental with its colours and application, creating an impressive royal image when on parade, attending banquets or meeting dignitaries. His appearance was particularly important; he was a young king and needed to present himself as a king and a man to be feared, respected and obeyed.

CHAPTER 5

Diplomat and warrior

When he came to the throne Tutankhamun was incredibly young to be king; he therefore needed a strong government of carefully-chosen officials and advisors behind him. Naturally, the young king chose many officials from the court of his father, Akhenaten. They possibly lived in Akhetaten during his childhood and been early influences on the young king; choosing them may have added an element of stability to his life. The most important officials were Ay, Horemheb and Maya, who remained prominent throughout his reign and were instrumental in many of his decisions. It is thought these three officials were the advisors behind all of Tutankhamun's political ideas and innovations.

Ay was the oldest and may have been involved heavily in the upbringing of the young king. He is believed to have been Tutankhamun's great uncle, the brother of Queen Tiye, son of Yuya and Thuya and possibly the father of Nefertiti, Akhenaten's wife. These family connections placed Ay high in the court of Akhenaten at Akhetaten; when Tutankhamun became king, Ay was one of his few relatives still alive. It was inevitable that he would hold a prominent position in the court of Tutankhamun. A box from either Amarna or Gurob lists Ay's titles, which include 'General of the Charioteer Corps', 'God's Father' and 'Overseer of the King's

House',[1] 'Fan Bearer on Right Hand of the King', 'Overseer of all the
Horses of his Majesty' and 'True Royal Scribe, Beloved of Him'[2]
under Akhenaten, 'Leader of the Festival of the Ennead',[3] (an hon-
orary title bestowed by the king) and 'Vizier' under Tutankhamun.
The Vizier was the most important administrative position in the
country, controlling the palace, taxes, national security and justice.

It has been suggested that in his early years, Ay was the young
prince's tutor.[4] If this was so, he may have been responsible for
teaching him about administration, politics and diplomacy: essen-
tially, how to be king. Tutankhamun's military training, although
within Ay's jurisdiction, especially considering his charioteering
skills, may have been overseen by General Horemheb.

Horemheb maintained his position as general in the armies of
Akhenaten, Tutankhamun and Ay. Although not in a position of
great power at Akhetaten, he was there and probably known to the
young prince. While living at Akhetaten, it is believed that he was
known as Paatenemheb (meaning 'Aten is in Festival'); a small
tomb in this name was started here, showing Paatenemheb held
similar military titles to Horemheb. He may have changed his
name to Horemheb (Horus is in Festival) to assert his religious
beliefs and to distance himself from the Aten cult and Akhenaten
after Tutankhamun ascended to the throne. While at Amarna,
Horemheb was married to a woman called Amenia; she is buried in
his Memphite tomb together with his second wife, Mutnodjmet.
Tutankhamun would probably not have known Amenia but
Mutnodjmet was Nefertiti's sister and lived at the Amarnan court
where he was brought up. She may even have resided at the North
Palace with the rest of the women. There are numerous images of
her at the court, apparently unmarried and often accompanied by
two dwarf attendants.[5] She probably helped care for the six daughters of her sister Nefertiti and probably Tutankhamun as well.

During the reigns of Akhenaten and Tutankhamun, Horemheb
was an important member of the army; his military career is recorded

in his Memphite tomb. The scribal skills achieved at the start of his career meant that Horemheb held a peacetime administrative role in the army at Akhetaten, in control of rotas, dossiers and military records. At Akhetaten, the military was primarily concerned with the protection of the king and, to a lesser extent, the city. Foreign relations were neglected during Akhenaten's reign, so it is unlikely that foreign campaigns were a major part of Horemheb's early military career. However, in year 12 (1338 BCE) of Akhenaten there was a Hittite rebellion and a small military campaign, the only one of the reign, which was probably led by Horemheb. During Tutankhamun's reign, Horemheb was 'Commander' of the Egyptian army, although probably primarily an administrative position. The only battles he possibly led were in the later years of Tutankhamun's reign against the Asiatics and the Nubians, but far from being idle, Horemheb worked his way through the ranks of officialdom to gain the revered title of 'Deputy King' under Tutankhamun.

It would seem that Horemheb had a lot of influence with the young king and may have been part of Tutankhamun's childhood at Akhetaten. Horemheb's coronation statue records his influence over the king and states that he was called to pacify the 'palace' (a euphemism for the king), when he 'had fallen into a rage'. It further states that only Horemheb could answer back to the king without fear of retribution and was the only one who could calm the king: 'he had but to open his mouth and answer the king to calm him with his speech'. This influence gave Horemheb power and status. To a small boy, Horemheb would have been a very impressive figure, to whom Tutankhamun looked up, admired and had a desire to emulate. Inscriptions on door jambs in the tomb of Horemheb at Memphis describe his elevated status:

Greater than the great ones, mightier than the mighty ones, great chieftain of the subjects ... who follows the king on his journeys in the southern and northern foreign land ... chief of

the most important courtiers, who listens to the confidences of
the unique ones ... master of the secrets of the Palace.

Horemheb is depicted in his Memphite tomb officiating over ceremonies of gold distribution, which was a typical Amarnan image.
The image depicts the king at a Window of Appearances throwing
gold collars to favoured courtiers. He is also shown being awarded
gold collars, possibly by Tutankhamun, for his services to Egypt.
Horemheb is shown in attendance at the coronation of King Ay,
which shows his continued loyalty to the royal family. He is
depicted at the coronation, looking after a group of foreign dignitaries, including Libyans, Western Asians, Nubians and Aegeans,
all pledging allegiance to the new king. The new king Ay then
appears at a Window of Appearances, giving tokens of achievement to the most favoured of his officials; no doubt one of them
was Horemheb, as shortly after this Ay named him heir to the
throne (he succeeded the throne upon Ay's death four years later).

Another important official was Maya, the 'Overseer of the
Treasury' under Tutankhamun, Ay and Horemheb. He may have
held a lower administrative position in Armana, enabling him to
become close to the royal family. Maya held his high position for
nearly twenty years and was clearly a trusted and competent official.

Although Ay was principal Vizier, Tutankhamun had another
two viziers during his reign who were carefully chosen and obviously trusted individuals. Usermont was one of these other viziers,
attested by a stela at Armana showing his role in the court of
Tutankhamun.[6]

He also held the titles 'Hereditary Prince, Governor, Mayor,
Vizier and Judge. The one whose utterance makes all the land con-
tent. The one of the curtain. The mouth of Hierokonpolis. The
Prophet of Maat and the Chief of the Great Mansions'. These show
that he held a prominent position in the court of Tutankhamun.
The other vizier was Penthu, who before his promotion held the

titles 'King's scribe, he who is at the head of the king, the chief servitor of Aten in the Mansion of Aten in Akhetaten, Chief physician', indicating he was a prominent figure in the court of Akhetaten, when the young Tutankhamun was growing up. As chief physician, Penthu may have treated the young prince and princesses for minor childhood ailments and may even have been the physician who treated the various members of the royal family for the illnesses that eventually led to their deaths.

Tutankhamun's first major diplomatic decision was to move the capital back to the traditional cities of Memphis and Thebes. The move away from Amarna saw the start of the restoration of the traditional culture and religion of Egypt, and the beginning of a campaign to destroy the monuments of Akhenaten. This must have seemed strange advice to the young king, as he had never known anything other than the cult of his father. However, he had to make a public show of restoring the damage caused by Akhenaten and eliminating the existence of the heretic king. As a traditional king, he re-used masonry blocks from his father's monuments to build his own; a number of recycled *talatat* blocks have been discovered at Karnak in the second and ninth pylons. They were originally used in the temple of Aten built by Akhenaten at Karnak, which Tutankhamun dismantled and had the blocks re-carved to use in his mortuary temple on the west bank at Thebes. At Karnak, Tutankhamun also erected the *Restoration Stela*, which outlined some of the plans he initiated to re-establish the cults and traditions of Egypt. As he was very young, it is likely that Horemheb or Ay contributed greatly to this text.

He is the effective King who did what was good for his father and all the gods. He restored everything that was ruined, to be his monument forever and ever. He has vanquished chaos from the whole land and has restored Maat to her place. He has made lying a crime, the whole land being made as it was at the time of Creation.

Now when His Majesty was crowned King the temples and the estates of the gods and goddesses from Elephantine as far as the swamps of Lower Egypt had fallen into ruin. Their shrines had fallen down, turned into piles of rubble and overgrown with weeds. Their sanctuaries were as if they had never existed at all. Their temples had become footpaths. The world was in chaos and the gods had turned their backs on this land. If an army was sent to *Djahy* to extend the boundaries of Egypt, it would have no success. If you asked a god for advice, he would not attend; and if one spoke to a goddess likewise she would not attend. Hearts were faint in bodies because everything that had been, was destroyed.

Now some days after this His Majesty appeared upon the throne of his father and he ruled the 'Two Banks of Horus', the Black Land and the Red Land being under his authority and every land bowed down before his might. Now His Majesty was in his palace which was in the House of Aakheperkare, being like the Sun in the sky and his Majesty carried out the works of this land and everything the Two Lands needed every day. Then His Majesty considered in his heart and looked for something which would be effective for his father Amun. He made the holy statue out of genuine electrum, giving to it more than had been done before. He made his father Amun 13 poles long, the holy statue being made of electrum, lapis lazuli, turquoise and every noble and precious stone, although the Majesty of this holy god had only been 11 poles long before. He also made Ptah-south-of-his-wall, Lord of Memphis, his holy statue of electrum, 11 poles long, the holy statue being made of electrum, lapis lazuli, turquoise and every noble and precious stone, when the Majesty of this noble god had been only seven poles long before. His Majesty made monuments for the gods, making their statues from electrum from the tribute of the foreign lands. He renewed their sanctuaries as his monuments forever and ever, endowing them with offerings forever, laying aside for them divine offerings daily, laying aside bread from the earth. He added great wealth on to that which existed before, doing more than his predecessors had ever done. He allocated *wab*-priests, God's Servants and the heirs of the Chiefs of the Cities to be the sons of wise men whose reputation is established. He has enriched their tables with gold and silver, bronze and copper without limit. He has filled their storehouses with male and female workers and with His Majesty's booty. He has added to the wealth of every temple, doubling, trebling and quadrupling the silver, gold, lapis lazuli, turquoise and every noble precious stone, together with *byssus*, white linen, ordinary linen, oil, fat, resin, incense, perfumes and myrrh without limit.

His Majesty ... has made quays for the river from new wood from the hill-slopes from the pick of Negau, inlaid with gold, the tribute of foreign countries, so that they might decorate the river. His majesty, Life Prosperity Health, picked male and female servants, musicians and dancers who had been women of the palace, their cost being charged to the palace and to the treasury of the two lands. I shall have them protected and guarded for my ancestors, the gods, in the hope that they will be contented, by doing what their *kas* wish while they protect Egypt.

Now the gods and goddesses of this land are rejoicing in their hearts, the Lords of the temples are in joy, the provinces all rejoice and celebrate throughout this whole land because good has come back into existence. The Ennead in the temple, their arms are raised in adoration, their hands are filled with jubilees forever and ever. All life and might is with them and it is for the nose of the mighty King Horus, repeater of births, beloved son of his father Amun, Lord of the gods, who made the one who made him, the King of Upper and Lower Egypt, his eldest son, the true and beloved one who protects his father who begot him.

His kingship is that of his father Osiris son of Re, the son who is good to the one who begot him, plentiful in monuments, rich in wonders, the one who makes an accurate monument for his father Amun, fair of births, the King who has established Egypt.[7]

Tutankhamun reinstated traditional festivals, including the cult of the Apis bull at Memphis. There was an Apis funeral during his lifetime, attested by a set of canopic jars dated to his reign. He also instigated the reinstatement of the cult of Horemakhet, the god of the sphinx and at Luxor temple an image depicts the 'Beautiful Opet Festival', an annual Theban festival stated by some to be the highlight of his reign. During the Opet Festival, the statue of Amun was removed from Karnak and taken in procession to the temple of Amun at Luxor (two kilometres away) during the second month of

Figure 15 *Tutankhamun's empty chariot at the Opet Festival. Luxor Temple. Photograph courtesy of Dave Thompson.*

Figure 16 *Tutankhamun making offerings to Amun. Luxor Temple. Photograph courtesy of Dave Thompson.*

the inundation. It was primarily a festival of fertility and rejuvenation of the king and a statement to the public that Tutankhamun possessed traditional kingly values (Figure 15). Tutankhamun depicted the entire festival and procession on the western wall of the pillared corridor at Luxor, between the first and the second pillared hall. Before the procession started, Tutankhamun made generous offerings of flowers, libations and incense to the god Amun, to appease him before his long journey (Figure 16) to the temple of Luxor. The journey between Karnak and Luxor followed the processional way or 'Sphinx Avenue' and the return journey was a river procession, with

Figure 17 *Military parade at the Opet Festival. Photograph courtesy of Dave Thompson.*

the divine boat towed by smaller sailing boats. The royal barge accompanied the sacred barques during the Nile procession.

The procession was accompanied by the Egyptian army who ran along the banks and were responsible for towing the royal barge (Figure 17). There was a wonderful atmosphere of celebration during this festival as a parade of singers, dancers (Figure 18) and dignitaries followed the god on his journey. The streets and the Nile were lined with an adoring public, eager to get a glimpse of the sacred barque or of the young boy king they thought might be the answer to the problems caused by Akhenaten. This was the first

Figure 18 *Dancers in the Opet Festival. Photograph courtesy of Dave Thompson.*

time the festival had taken place for nearly a decade and signalled the end of a dark period. Once again the people were allowed to worship the gods of their choice and Amun was restored as 'King of the Gods'. The singers accompanying the procession sang songs of praise to Amun and songs to entertain the crowds:

> There is a welcoming inn
> Its awning facing south
> There is a welcoming inn
> Its awning facing north
> Drink, sailors of the king
> Beloved of Amun
> Praised of the gods[8]

This gives some idea of the festivities that accompanied this very religious festival. The people revelled and feasted for the eleven days that the statue of Amun remained in the sanctuary of Luxor, celebrating the journey of the god, the rejuvenation of the king and the ideologies of kingship.

The end of the first Opet Festival during the reign of Tutankhamun left the population of Thebes full of hope for the future and probably of disappointment that after eleven days of festivities they had to return to work and their normal lives. The Opet Festival was a very important aspect of Tutankhamun's re-establishment of the traditional religion, values and traditions and endeared this young child to the population of Thebes as their salvation from the politically and religiously unstable period that had just passed. These representations of the Opet Festival at Luxor were later usurped by Horemheb, giving the impression that it was he who had restored this festival to the people of Thebes (Figure 19).

Figure 19 *Tutankhamun at Luxor. The cartouche is Horemheb's. Luxor Temple. Photograph courtesy of Dave Thompson.*

To enable the restoration of the religious cults and reinstatement of Memphis and Thebes as the capitals, Tutankhamun needed to raise taxes. This ensured the royal coffers remained full and the restoration could be completed. A stela (currently in the School of Archaeology and Oriental Studies at the University of Liverpool, UK) describes Maya's order to collect some of these taxes:

Year 8, third month of Peret season, day 22, under the majesty of Horus, Mighty Bull, Pleasing of Birth; Nebti, Good of Laws, Who Pacifies the Two Lands; Golden Horus, who Lifts up the Crowns and who Satisfies the gods; the King of Upper and Lower Egypt, Nebkheperure, Son of Re, Tutankhamun, Given life.

On this day, His Majesty commanded the hereditary prince and count, the fan bearer on the right hand of the king, royal scribe, Overseer of the treasury, Maya, justified to tax the entire land and to institute divine offerings for all the gods of the land of Egypt, beginning from Elephantine as far as Sma-neb-Behdet (*Delta*).

An offering which the king gives to [...] protector of his father, tha they may give [...] daily and a happy lifetime and a good burial after old age until reaching the necropolis, for the *ka* of the hereditary prince, count, fan bearer of the sole lord who is among [...] real royal scribe, whom he loves, Overseer of the Treasury, Maya.[9]

It is clear that the taxes collected were to go towards the reinstating of the traditional gods, religion and, in particular, offerings and rituals. Unfortunately, we do not know where this stela was erected, whether it was in his funerary chapel or on one of Tutankhamun's monuments. It is thought it was probably either erected at the start of the journey, in Elephantine, or at the temple of Amun at Karnak.[10] What we do know is that this event was important enough to warrant the use of a piece of sandstone to record it. This tax collection happened in January or February 1337 BCE, the best time, climatically, to start the long journey from Elephantine in the south. As Maya was instructed to go and collect the taxes personally throughout the whole of Egypt, this suggests it was either a particularly important mission or one that could produce problems which could only be rectified by the Treasurer himself. If this were the first tax collection of its kind, Tutankhamun perhaps expected retaliation from the people, which would require the soothing words of a superior government official. It is more likely that Maya was sent on this mission because he was trustworthy. At this unstable time, corruption was probably rife amongst the lower officials and Tutankhamun wanted to ensure the taxes reached the royal coffers to pay for the restorations and not the pocket of a dishonest tax-collector. The level of government corruption is mentioned in the Edict of Horemheb, a text which describes the crimes and corruption in Egypt at the start of his reign and the measures he undertook to return to the peaceful time of the reign of Amenhotep III. It is also possible that there was a certain amount of uncertainty about religion after the tyrannical insistence of Akhenaten that everyone should worship the Aten. Maya was sent to ensure that the rituals were being carried out in the temples but also to reassure the people that worship of the traditional gods was now actively encouraged by the king and his royal court.

As part of his campaign, Tutankhamun started a number of building projects, including extensive work at the Luxor and Karnak temples, dedicated to the god Amun. He commissioned so many monuments that an epithet on the stamp on his tomb door refers to him as he 'who spent his life in fashioning images of the gods' (Figure 19). The Restoration Stela outlines the building works that Tutankhamun initiated at the start of his reign:

> He made the holy statue out of genuine electrum, giving to it more than had been done before. He made his father Amun 13 poles long, the holy statue being made of electrum, lapis lazuli, turquoise and every noble and precious stone, although the Majesty of this holy god had been only 11 poles long

Figure 20 *Tutankhamun as Amun. Luxor Museum. Photograph courtesy of Wayne Frostick.*

before . . . His Majesty made monuments for the gods, making their statues from electrum from the tribute of the foreign lands. He renewed their sanctuaries as his monuments forever and ever, endowing them with offerings forever, laying aside for them divine offerings daily, laying aside bread from the earth. He added great wealth on to that which existed before, doing more than his predecessors had ever done.

Figure 21 *Tutankhamun's sphinx from the sphinx avenue. Photograph courtesy of Dave Thompson.*

Tutankhamun focused most of his building works in Thebes, the main cult centre of the god Amun. Because he wanted to associate himself with Amenhotep III rather than Akhenaten, he continued the building works of his grandfather. At Karnak, the processional sphinx avenue from the tenth pylon to the complex of Mut, originally erected by Amenhotep III, was improved by Tutankhamun, his contribution consisting of a number of ram-headed sphinxes.[11] One solitary sphinx, bearing the face of Tutankhamun, is still

Figure 22 *Tutankhamun protected by Amun. Louvre Museum, Paris. Photograph courtesy of Wayne Frostick.*

visible in the first court of the main temple at Karnak (Figure 21). Tutankhamun also constructed a number of statues to Amun at Karnak, all bearing his face (Figures 22 and 23) and statues of the divine consort Mut, bearing the face of his wife Ankhesenamun (Figure 24). He started a programme of decoration of the eastern enclosure wall of the *cachette* court and built two shrines referred to as the 'temple of Nebkheperure, beloved of Amun, established in Thebes' and the 'Temple of Nebkheperure in Thebes'. Only fragmentary remains exist of these shrines. The decoration from these shrines consists of inscriptions of both Tutankhamun and

Figure 23 *Tutankhamun group statue. Karnak Temple. Photograph courtesy of Dave Thompson.*

Ay, images of a royal funeral (probably that of Tutankhamun) and a hunting scene showing the king in his chariot, firing arrows at desert game. Other scenes from a door lintel show Tutankhamun in traditional pose, offering libations to Amun and his consort Mut, the deities of Karnak.

The agricultural ceremony of the 'Driving of the Calves' is also depicted here. In this ceremony, the young calves are paraded before the god Amun, a display of the wealth of Egypt and in gratitude to the god.[12] The king depicted in this scene appears to

Figure 24 *Tutankhamun and Ankhesenamun as Amun and Mut. Luxor Temple. Photograph courtesy of Dave Thompson.*

be Ay, as most of the decoration was completed during his reign and he takes credit for building this structure in honour of Tutankhamun.[13] He claims that Tutankhamun is his son, although strangely this has not generated the same amount of discussion as the Soleb lions, where Tutankhamun called Amenhotep III his father (See Chapter 3). It is taken as read that Ay refers to Tutankhamun as his son to associate himself with him and his monuments and legitimise his right to the throne.[14]

Tutankhamun continued work at the temple of Luxor by completing the colonnade and the decoration, as well as adding blocks to the temples of Thutmosis III at Medinet Gurob, Abydos and the Faiyum. All these construction projects reinforced the ideology of kingship and reasserted the presence of the king throughout Egypt, reassuring the people that he was restoring Egypt back to 'normal'. Tutankhamun then travelled to the Nubian temple of Amenhotep III at Soleb and expanded the temple there. Two red granite lions from this temple are currently in the British Museum; one bears the inscription which refers to Amenhotep III as his father and is an important factor in the debate on his parentage. He also built temples to his own divine cult at Faras and Kawa in Nubia.

Although the Faras temple has now been totally destroyed, the small cult temple at Kawa is still standing. It was dedicated to two forms of the god Amun; the Amun of Karnak and a local form. This local form of Amun is believed to have been an incarnation of Tutankhamun and continued the tradition of his family; the local form of Amun at Soleb was Amenhotep III and the local Hathor of Sedeinga was Tiye. By deifying himself at Kawa, Tutankhamun was further associating himself with the traditions of Amenhotep III and distancing himself from Akhenaten and his teachings. The sister of the Viceroy of Kush, Taemwadjsi, held the title of the 'Chief of the Harem of the Deified Tutankhamun' in addition to the more mortal harem at his palace, indicating the universality of this cult.[15] A roughly carved stela of her brother, Huy, discovered at Karnak, dedicated to the deified Tutankhamun, suggests this cult was carried as far as the Theban region. The powers attributed to the deified Tutankhamun on this stela are interesting. Huy dedicated the stela to Amun-Re, a ram-headed Amun and the *ka* of Tutankhamun. He appeals to the *ka* to deliver him from the blindness with which he has afflicted. Whether this is real blindness or a spiritual blindness as punishment for a sin is uncertain but appealing to the king for help shows he was considered something more than mortal.[16] This attributes the power of punishment and forgiveness on this young boy king. These things are still being attributed to him in the form of the curse, although many of the curse supporters do not refer to the deification of the king or the powers the Egyptians attributed to him.

Tutankhamun built a smaller sanctuary in Nubia, in a town known as 'He who appeases the gods', dedicated to the traditional gods Amun, Amun-Ra, Re-Horakhty and the cult of the king himself, reinforcing the national status of the cult of his deified form. This region of Nubia formed the centre of Nubian administration, from which Tutankhamun and his newly appointed Viceroy of Kush, Huy, controlled the import of Nubian goods into Egypt, in particular gold, strengthening the Egyptian economy. The temples erected by Tutankhamun re-established the Egyptian presence in Nubia. In addition to the Viceroy Huy, there were other Egyptian officials in Napata, a city near the fourth cataract. Huy had two assistants, one of whom was named Amunemipet. Huy and his assistants held the royal seal and a lot of power in the region. He was responsible for collecting taxes and tributes from the local Nubians; half was sent to Tutankhamun's treasurer Maya in Thebes and the other half remained in Nubia for redistribution as rations to the Egyptian military and officials stationed there.

Returning to Thebes, like all kings before him, Tutankhamun built a mortuary temple on the west bank of the Nile. The foundations of this temple have not been clearly identified, although the location, just north of the Medinet Habu temple of Ramses III, is clear (Figure 25). Two colossal statues of Tutankhamun were found in the remains of the mortuary temples of Ay and Horemheb and it is thought that his temple lies beneath theirs. Evidence of the funerary priests of the cult of the *ka* of Tutankhamun indicates that he definitely built a mortuary temple which, for a short time at least, was in full working order.[17]

Although he focused most of his building works in Thebes and the south of Egypt, there is evidence of building works in Memphis, the ancient capital of Egypt. An inscription belonging to

Figure 25 *Medinet Habu temple. The mortuary temple of Tutankhamun/Ay/Horemheb would be in the centre right of the picture, near the rear of Medinet Habu. Photograph courtesy of Wayne Frostick.*

'the scribe of the Treasury of the Domain of Tutankhamun' in Memphis indicates that Tutankhamun built some administrative buildings in this region and re-established the site as the administrative capital, moving it away from Amarna.[18] One structure built by Tutankhamun in Memphis was a palace called the 'House of Nebkheperure';[19] it is thought that the Restoration Stela may have been issued from this palace and set up in Thebes.[20] Other evidence of Tutankhamun in the north is scarce, due to the nature of archaeological evidence in this region.

One piece of evidence of Tutankhamun in the north is a stela discovered near the Sphinx. The stela is broken in two but shows Tutankhamun and Ankhesenamun with a figure bowing down before them. This figure has been erased but he was bent at the waist in traditional Amarnan style. The stela was set up by the courtier depicted, although his name is now missing, to show his loyalty to the new king. It is thought that as he is holding a fan over his right shoulder he could represent a 'royal fan-bearer'; Horemheb, Maya and Nakhtmin all held this title. Nakhtmin was a royal scribe, fan bearer on the right hand of the king and a general in the army, so also a colleague of Horemheb. It is clear that he was close to Tutankhamun throughout his reign and he placed a statue in his tomb as a final gift, inscribed with the words 'the servant who makes his master's name live'.[21] It has been suggested that images where a fan is held over the head of the king represent his divinity and so this stela could reflect the spread of the cult of the deified Tutankhamun (and the reverence of the king of the dedicator of the stela) as far north as Memphis.[22] Unfortunately, this brings us no closer to identifying the owner of this stela.

There are only two parallel examples of a courtier paying homage in this manner from this reign, both of Ay: a stela from Karnak and a strip of gold showing Ay adoring his king. However, if it is Tutankhamun, it would be the only image of Ay and Tutankhamun together on a monument from Memphis and is therefore thought not to represent him. The only other definite attestations of Tutankhamun in Memphis are the door jamb from the hunting lodge from the region of the sphinx which names him and his wife and the reused door jamb which refers to Hathor as the 'Chief of the West of Memphis', indicating it was originally erected in that region, perhaps as part of a chapel to Hathor.[23] The door jambs retain traces of Tutankhamun's cartouches, indicating he originally built it.

From this interesting portfolio of monumental structures, it seems Tutankhamun earned his epithet of he 'who spent his life in fashioning images of the gods', for all this was achieved in only ten years of rule. Bearing in mind that a number of his monuments are attested purely by textual reference, with no knowledge of their location, this young king probably built more monuments that have yet to be uncovered by archaeology.

During his reign, Tutankhamun spent much of his time meeting dignitaries and building diplomatic bridges between nations. Although Egypt was economically weak and religiously unstable when he came to the throne, foreign relations were quite positive. In the reign of Amenhotep III, foreign relations had been well-maintained; the Amarna letters demonstrate the strong relationships between Amenhotep and foreign rulers, strengthened by the process of gift-giving. Akhenaten initially maintained these relationships but some of the Amarna letters suggest that he neglected foreign policy in favour of his new religion and his new city. Unfortunately, at this time, the Hittite army was marching through the Near East, murdering the supporters and vassal kings of Egypt. The letters show that the vassal rulers pleaded with Akhenaten to send the Egyptian army to defend them but these pleas fell on deaf ears, resulting in their deaths at the hands of the Hittites. A scene in the tomb of Horemheb at Memphis shows Asiatics begging Tutankhamun for aid after what may have been the Hittite invasion of their land:

'The barbarians have taken their land, their dwellings have been destroyed, their towns devastated and their crops burnt. Their country has been so hungry that they lived in the mountains like goats. Now they come to beg the powerful to send his victorious sword to protect them, saying 'we few Asiatics who do not know how we may survive have come to seek refuge in the land of pharaoh as we did in the time of the fathers of his father, since the beginning'.[24]

Unfortunately, due to the damage in the tomb, we do not know exactly what Tutankhamun did to help these people but as it was recorded for posterity, it is likely he responded favourably and allowed the Asiatic community to settle in Egypt. Many foreigners were similarly accepted into the Egypt and given a home, land and work depending on their skills; they might be manual labourers, shipbuilders, physicians, fan bearers or butlers.[25]

In Tutankhamun's tomb were many items which were probably gifts from foreign kings. It is quite likely these gifts were presented formally, in the palace of the king, perhaps by the foreign kings themselves or by delegates on behalf of their ruler. For such receptions, probably at Malkata, Tutankhamun sat on his throne, on a raised dais approached by a short flight of steps. On the steps were images of bound captives, scenes designed to show Egypt's dominance and intimidate the visiting dignitaries. As he was a young boy, Tutankhamun's throne was specially made to fit him. A child-sized throne and footstool were placed in the tomb; it is possible this was his actual throne (Plate 11). The throne is in ebony, with gilded armrests and ivory inlays in the backrest. The chair stands on four feet carved in the shape of lions' paws, complete with gilded claws. The low, matching footstool ensured the king's feet did not touch the floor.

When Tutankhamun became king he strove to improve foreign relations, especially with the Mittanni, which had completely disintegrated during the reign of Akhenaten. (Mittanni was a Hurrian kingdom in Mesopotamia, in modern Syria.) There appear to be more Mitannian diplomatic gifts in his tomb than those from other nations. If Tadukhipa, the Mitannian princess married to his father, was Tutankhamun's mother, the relationship between Egypt and Mitanni would be particularly strong. Even if she were not his mother, she may still have been alive. It is also possibilite that the Mitannian king sent a bride to Tutankhamun to seal an alliance between the two countries and these 'gifts' formed part of a dowry.

The Mittannian diplomatic gifts were varied but clearly personal and intimate items, showing a close relationship between the two rulers. They included a pair of leather sandals of the type mentioned in the Amarna letters. These 'foreign' shoes have a toe loop and are filled in at the back, unlike Egyptian shoes which were more like modern flip-flops (Plate 13). Several linen socks were also found, with separate toes and fastenings along the front like shoe laces. These were also probably of foreign origin, as socks and shoes were generally not worn in Egypt, due to the very hot climate. When Tutankhamun was around twelve to fourteen years old (judging by the size) the Mittannian king sent him a tunic, elaborately embroidered with his names and titles. Less intimate gifts probably of Mittanian origin included a silver dagger blade, a valuable item, as silver was not native to Egypt. A matching iron dagger (also unavailable in Egypt) may have formed a set with the silver example. There was also a bracelet, set with a large amethyst scarab; again, amethyst is not native to Egypt. These objects are more typical of diplomatic gifts, whereas the personal clothing indicates a more intimate relationship. For the young king, re-establishing this relationship after a period of neglect would have been difficult and could indicate the maturing of his diplomatic skills, under the tutelage of Ay, Maya and Horemheb.

Items from other foreign countries show Tutankhamun worked at his international relations. The weave of some of the decorative collars on his tunics, examined closely, has shown they were not produced in Egypt but came from Ethiopia, probably as diplomatic gifts. Tutankhamun also had a Syrian-style hip wrap, 2.1 metres in length, trimmed with a red braid on each edge and two bands down the centre. This was wrapped one and a half times around the body and held in place by a sash. It may have been a diplomatic gift from a Syrian leader or may have been part of the booty captured during the Syrian military campaign of the later years of his reign. Either way, it seems unlikely that he ever wore it except in games of 'dressing up'.

Evidence indicates that in the last three years of his reign (1327–1324 BCE) Tutankhamun accepted a visit from a foreign delegation which finalised the re-establishment of trade relations between Egypt, Babylonia and Assyria. Letters from the Amarna archive show that Burnaburiash, the king of Babylonia, requested gifts from Tutankhamun. However, he held back from giving them, due to Egypt's complicated relations with the Assyrians, who Burnaburiash greatly feared. One Amarna letter, believed by some scholars to date to the reign of Tutankhamun, suggests the king was trying to manipulate Assyria and Babylonia in favour of Egypt. If it was sent to Tutankhamun, he was playing complicated politics for a young boy. The letter reads:

To Niphuria, King of Egypt, spoken by Burnaburiash, King of Babylonia, your brother.

All goes well for me. All hail to you, your house, your wives, your children, your country, your nobles, your horses and your chariots. When my fathers and your fathers established between themselves friendly relations they exchanged rich presents and never refused each other, the one to the other, whatever beautiful thing they desired.

Now my brother has sent me as a gift only two *minas* of gold. If gold is now abundant with you, send me as much as your fathers did but if it is scarce, send me at least half of it. Why did you send me only two *minas* of gold?

Now the tasks I have to carry out in the temple are great and I have undertaken them with zeal to accomplish them; therefore send me much gold.

As for you, whatever you desire of the produce of my country, write to me and it shall be brought to you. At the time of Kurigalzu, my father, the Canaanites all together wrote to him: 'we are going to the frontier of the country in order to cross it, that is why we wish to enter into relations with you'.

Here is what my father replied to them: 'Abandon any idea of making an alliance with me! If you perform hostile deeds against the king of Egypt, my brother, in league with others, is it not I who will have to go and punish you since he is allied to me?' It was for your father's sake that my father did not listen to them.

Now concerning the Assyrians, my vassals, I have written nothing to you as they claim. Why have they gone to your country? If you love me, they must not be allowed to buy anything at all. Let them return here empty-handed!

It is as a present of friendship that I send to you three measures of beautiful lapis lazuli stone and also five teams of horses for five wooden chariots.[26]

It would appear from this letter that the Egyptian king, possibly Tutankhamun, promised gifts to Burnaburiash and in the mean time received the Assyrian nobles in his palace at Thebes. The Assyrians and the Babylonians clearly did not trust each other. The Assyrians made claims against the Babylonians to the Egyptians, which Burnaburiash feels the need to deny 'I have written nothing to you as they claim'. The king obviously wanted to have both the Assyrians and the Babylonians as vassals, as this would make Egypt a much more powerful force in the Near East. He hoped to keep his Assyrian dealings from the Babylonians, so the king of Babylonia would shower him with gifts as a means of showing more loyalty than the Assyrians. It would be interesting to know what the next stage in these double-dealings would have been. Would the Assyrians be encouraged to give further gifts, to outshine the Babylonian king, and so on, until Egypt felt it had got what it desired? This probably would have worked quite well if the Babylonian king had not discovered the double-dealing. Sadly, this is the only letter that could be dated to Tutankhamun's reign, so other such dealings are now lost.

Although Tutankhamun spent much of his reign restoring religious, economic and political relations, it also appears that he participated in at least two battles in the later years of his short royal career, one against the Asiatics and one against the Nubians. These were recorded at his mortuary temple on the west bank of Thebes and although the temple is no longer standing, some of the blocks have been recovered from the pylons of the temple of Karnak. These blocks were first thought to have come from the 'Temple of Nebkheperure (*Tutankhamun*) in Thebes', although it is now agreed that they originated in his mortuary temple.[27] The blocks were re-used from the Karnak temples of Akhenaten by Tutankhamun and then Ay. Some of the blocks bear the cartouche of Tutankhamun, making it clear that they were from his reign. The battle scenes flanked a doorway of the mortuary temple, the Nubian battle on the left and the Asiatic battle on the right, representing his dominance over both the northern and southern territories.

As Tutankhamun was so young, some suggest that he may not have taken part in the battle himself but merely accompanied the army to the battlefield, to provide moral support and motivation for the troops. Military furniture was placed in his tomb, including a travel bed, which folded into a Z-shape on copper hinges, and

folding stools (Plate 14) used on campaigns which could be transported easily. There was also a set of body armour: a close fitting
bodice without sleeves, similar to Asiatic scale-armour and possibly another diplomatic gift. We will never know if he wore this in
battle, although other kings are depicted in this type of armour.
The earliest depictions are on the alabaster chapel of Amenhotep I
at Karnak and a chariot of Thutmosis IV, both Tutankhamun's
ancestors. Bronze scale-armour was also found at the palace of
Amenhotep III at Malkata, indicating it was worn during his
grandfather's reign. Tutankhamun may have worn it in the northern campaign or perhaps for protection while hunting.

A number of weapons were found in his tomb, including
swords, scimitars, slings and throw-sticks. There were also eight
shields, indicating that if he did not actually go to war he was at
least trained in the required skills. Strangely enough, although
there were six chariots in his tomb there were no war chariots, only
ceremonial and hunting vehicles. This could support the sugges-
tion that he did not participate in the battles, or it may be that the
war chariots belonged to the army and were kept for future kings,
not taken out of circulation by being placed in a tomb.

Further attestation of his military career comes from the
two military trumpets found in his tomb, one silver and one
copper or bronze (Plate 15). The silver trumpet, found carefully
wrapped in reeds, was made of beaten silver with a thin band of
gold decoration around the edge of the bell. This trumpet was
approximately 58 cm long.[28] The other trumpet, of copper or
bronze, is also decorated with a gold band but is shorter (approximately 50 cm) than the silver example.[29] It has a mouthpiece with a
silver band attached to the end of a tube. The metal of this example
will only be ascertained if it is ever chemically analysed. Both
trumpets were decorated with traditional motifs of Egyptian art,
including the names of Re-Horakhty, Amun-Re and Ptah and with
a scene showing Tutankhamun facing Amun and Re-Horakhty.

The gods are shown holding the *ankh* (sign of eternal life) to his nose. The divisions of the Egyptian army were named after a number of deities, the most important being Amun-Re, Re-Horakhty and Ptah, which suggests the image represents the king standing before his troops. The king's clothes in the image could represent a military uniform: he wears the blue, or war, crown, a kilt, collars and heavy bracelets. In his hand he holds the *hekat* (sceptre of magical power) perhaps representing the power and support of the gods that he would bring into a battle.[30]

The scenes appear to have been added to the trumpets after the written inscriptions. As plainer items, they would be less likely to be damaged on campaign and would be easier to repair. Adding the images may have been a way of turning a functional military instrument into a funerary object. To limit the damage travelling might cause to the instruments, they were fitted with wooden cores, both of which were discovered in the tomb. The cores were solid pieces of wood, identical in shape to the trumpets. It is believed they were made first and the sheet metal beaten around them to create the trumpet. It has been suggested that these cores may have been used to suspend the instruments, as they have suspension holes. However, once inserted into the trumpet the suspension hole would not be visible, which suggests that the cores were designed to be suspended when the instruments were in use, perhaps hung from the trumpeter's kilt.[31] The wooden cores may have been included in the tomb to complete the instrument as Tutankhamun would have known it, or as a means of muting them so they did not make any unwarranted noise before the resurrection of the king.[32]

Since the discovery of the tomb in 1922, archaeologists have been curious about what sound these instruments might make. In 1939, the silver trumpet was played by Bandsman James Tappern of the 11th Prince Albert's Own Hussars. Unfortunately, he used a modern mouthpiece; when he blew, the pressure shattered the silver trumpet into many pieces. After repairs, a second attempt to play them was made in 1975, by Philip Jones, a bass instrumentalist, in the Museum in Cairo.[33] He did not use a mouthpiece. The instruments produced haunting sounds, which were recorded. The silver trumpet could play C, G and E and the copper trumpet D, C and B; a very limited note range. This limited range and the difficulty in reaching higher notes would suggest that these instruments were not used for music but as rhythmic accompaniment to marching or for signalling on the battleground.[34]

The *talatat* blocks recovered from Tutankhamun's mortuary temple record four different, although fragmentary, episodes from his battles, with many parts of the battle narrative missing. Of the two battles, information on the Asiatic campaign is better preserved than the Nubian. If we assume Tutankhamun did not actively participate in the fighting, these campaigns would have been led by the army general and 'Deputy King', Horemheb. Horemheb's tomb at Saqqara has images of a northern and southern campaign, which are possibly the same battles. The Asiatics are depicted as coming from two different groups: Canaanites, with mushroom-shaped haircuts and beards, and Syrians, with cropped hair and full beards. The scenes start with the battle itself, which was fought on land using chariots. Egyptian chariots were lighter, swifter and more manoeuvrable than the Asiatic vehicles. They held two men, an archer or spear-bearer and a shield-bearer, whereas the Asiatic chariots held three, a driver, shield-bearer and archer. The king is shown in the centre of the battle scene, in his war-chariot, surrounded by his regiment of charioteers. They are pursuing the enemy chariots at speed and followed by the infantry, who are depicted running.

The battle images are graphic: Asiatics fall from their chariots with arrows and spears piercing their bodies and are dragged under the wheels of the Egyptian vehicles. One Asiatic charioteer has fallen from his chariot and has become tangled in his own

Figure 26 *Asiatics falling from the ramparts of their fortified town (after Johnson W.R. 1992, Figure 18). Illustration by Charlotte Booth.*

reins, helplessly dragged behind the moving chariot. The Asiatics are clearly terrified of the Egyptians: their chariot corps flies from the Egyptian army, closely followed by the Egyptian chariots. They were chased to a walled citadel, within which they hoped to barricade themselves, but the Egyptians placed scaling ladders against the walls to penetrate the fortress. From the bottom of the tower, they killed a number of Asiatics, who can be seen falling from the ramparts (Figure 26). From one of the lower ramparts, three Asiatic women and a small child are shown wailing and holding their arms aloft in fear of the Egyptian army and grieving for the loss of their kinsmen. The end scene shows the Egyptian victory. A pile of Asiatics are being killed, if not quite dead, or having their hands cut off by the Egyptian soldiers as a means of counting the

Figure 27 *Tutankhamun receiving booty after the battle (after Johnson W.R. 1992, Figure 20). Illustration by Charlotte Booth.*

enemy dead. The hands were counted and recorded by the military scribes; some of the soldiers are shown with hands threaded on to their spears as trophies for the victory parade (Figure 27).

The Nubian battle is very similar although the information is far more fragmentary. It was also a chariot battle, following the same 'plan' as the Asiatic battle and also with a victory parade. The details are equally graphic: one block shows a Nubian soldier trapped beneath a chariot wheel (Figure 28); if that were not enough, an Egyptian soldier is cutting off his hand. The next element of the battle is the presentation of booty and prisoners, probably by a general or high-ranking officer. The Nubian prisoners are manacled, with their hands attached to their necks, the first depiction of this device, regularly shown in the Ramesside period.[35] The soldiers presenting the prisoners bow down low or kneel, indicating they were in actual close proximity to the king, rather than it being a stylised image. Sadly, the identification of the captured booty is damaged but it included a floral vase and a small jug, which doubtless pleased the king. When all the prisoners and booty had

Figure 28 *A Nubian under the wheel in the Nubian battle. An Egyptian soldier cuts off his hand (after Johnson W.R. 1992, Figure 6). Illustration by Charlotte Booth.*

been presented the king presented them to the god Amun. Tutankhamun is depicted standing in a raised dais before the god Amun who is seated, possibly with Mut and Khonsu behind him. The king has the piles of booty in front of him and the rows of prisoners behind him. The god accepts the gifts.

The victory procession at the end of both battles was two-fold: on land and river. The processions were an important part of the battle. The land procession consisted of rows of chariots with the infantry marching alongside. During the Nubian parade, the soldiers marching in victory are depicted wearing the tasselled helmets of the Asiatics defeated in the previous battle and the soldiers from that battle have their spears threaded with enemy hands. The charioteers are shown walking alongside their plumed horses, clutching the reins. These chariot teams are accompanied by infantry, some holding battle axes and open fans. The king watched the procession from a raised dais, through a portable Window of Appearances, which was carried to the battlefield. The Window of Appearances was an aspect of his life at Amarna and closely associated with addressing the people. His empty chariot is just behind him in the image, showing he had just alighted and also that the procession took place in the field, rather than in a palace or temple. These small details suggest that this was a record of a real event, as they hold no religious or ideological significance. Tutankhamun stood at the window as piles of booty were placed in front of him, and the prisoners, bound together, were marched before him.

After the land procession, the Egyptian army made a spectacular, victorious return to Thebes in a river procession. Four towboats in full sail towed the royal barge, in full sail and with many rowers, at its head. On both sides of the Nile ran rows of infantry. To clarify the king's role in the battle and demonstrate the maintenance of order over chaos, a cage was hung from the royal barge with a Syrian prisoner within (Figure 29) and is the first time this device appears in artistic imagery, although it is mentioned in an Amenhotep II text on the punishment of chieftains of enemy tribes.[36] The Syrian could have been a chieftain; his presence would show the importance and prowess of Tutankhamun in capturing the leader of the enemy. Once the procession arrived in Thebes, the booty and prisoners were offered to Amun at the temple of Karnak.

A scene in the tomb of Horemheb at Memphis shows a number of foreign prisoners, both Asiatics and Nubians, being recorded by the military scribes. This probably represents the post-battle activities of these two campaigns. There may have been further scenes, describing the time before the battle started, including a scene showing the support of Amun as he hands the sword of victory to the young king. The northward journey of the king and his army would also have been depicted as a means of setting the scene, but unfortunately these scenes are lost. Perhaps the continuing work at Karnak on the *talatat* blocks will uncover the missing pieces.

For such a young king, Tutankhamun was clearly very active politically, involved in both peaceful and non-peaceful campaigns to

Figure 29 *The Syrian prisoner in a cage on the royal barge (after Johnson W.R. 1992, Figure 5). Illustration by Charlotte Booth.*

reassert the flagging power of Egypt in the Near East. The products of his campaigning were the strengthened relations between Mitanni, Ethiopia and the Assyrians, and Egypt's domination over Syria and Nubia. This would have made it clear to the surrounding countries that Egypt was once again a force to be reckoned with.

CHAPTER 6

The decade draws to a close

Despite the many innovations and changes instigated by the young boy king, he was cut down in his prime, dying when he was approximately eighteen or nineteen years old. How he died has long interested scholars and there are many theories. The highest recorded date for his reign is year 10 (1334 BCE);[1] the floral remains in his tomb show that he died in January and was buried seventy days later, in late March or April.[2]

Tutankhamun's mummy has been X-rayed twice since its discovery, once in 1968 by R.G. Harrison and again in 1978 by J.E. Harris. It was CT scanned in 2005. The 2005 CT scan says much about the general health of Tutankhamun when he was growing up as well as possibly enlightening us on the cause of his death. Initial studies showed his bones had no signs of malnutrition or infectious disease during his childhood, and that he was a well-fed healthy adult, living a good life, as would be expected of a king. Studies of his teeth have been difficult, because of the solidifying of the resin which covered his mummy. The available X-ray images show that he had one impacted wisdom tooth and that the others had not yet erupted, indicating he was between eighteen and twenty-two years old. When Dr Derry examined the body in 1925, he noted that the wisdom teeth were just erupting. Unfortunately,

as there were no X-rays then, Derry would only have known this by
cutting the underside of the chin and pulling the tongue down so
that he could see inside the mouth. To cover this desecration of the
royal body, he put the flap of skin back and covered it with resin so
it looked like the rest of the body.[3] It was impossible to investigate
the wear on his teeth but the X-rays show he did not suffer from
caries (decay) or abscesses.[4]

Most people in ancient Egypt had very bad teeth, by modern
standards, although caries were rare, due to the low sugar content
in their diet. However, most people suffered from extensive wear
to their teeth, because their bread contained sand or quartz due to
low quality flour or wind-blown particles entering the flour before
baking. This extensive wear was so extreme it exposed the pulp of
the tooth, which became infected and led to abscesses. There was
little relief from this ailment, other than having it drained using a
hollow reed and chewing on cloves to alleviate the pain. The young
king had not worn his teeth down to such an extent, so his mouth
was relatively healthy but no doubt, with age, his teeth would have
slowly deteriorated.

From the study of his body and other items in the tomb it is possible to get an impression of Tutankhamun's appearance. His
mummy shows he was of slight build, although he was healthy and
well-fed. He was 1.67 m (approximately five feet five inches) in
height, average for ancient Egyptian men.[5] The wooden man-
nequin in his tomb shows his chest measured 80 cm and items of
clothing in his tomb that his waist was 75 cm and his hips 108 cm.
This shows he had a relatively narrow waist, with large rounded
hips; it is possible he suffered from bilharzia or another infestation
which caused bodily changes. Bilhazia is a parasitic worm, caught
from water snails living in the Nile canals. Egyptians ancient and
modern, rich and poor suffered (and suffer) from this. It causes
anaemia, loss of appetite, urinary infection and loss of resistance to
other diseases, as well as abdominal swelling. There is also evidence

that he suffered from a mild cleft palate, which did not develop into a hare lip or other facial anomaly. He had large frontal incisors, giving him a substantial overbite (a characteristic of his family line) and his bottom teeth were uneven. His mummy was originally thought to show signs of scoliosis (curvature of the spine), although the CT scan in 2005 showed that this was probably due to the embalmers wrapping him while his spine was in an unnaturally curved position.

Various scientific studies have moulded the theories of his death. The 1968 study reported that Tutankhamun may have suffered a blow to the head, based on the discovery of two loose pieces of bone in his skull. This theory has dominated books and articles since. A thinning of the bone behind his left ear may have been caused by this blow to the head. The left leg and right knee cap were broken just before his death and he had many other fractures, occuring both post- and pre-death, suggesting to some that his death was the result of foul play. One theory is that the blow to the head, resulting in the thinning of the bone behind the ear, was a bungled murder attempt, which resulted in a slowly-developing tumour. Tutankhamun survived this blow for many months, living with the tumour, which caused headaches, dizziness and possible periods of immobility. He mentioned his symptoms to the physicians, who sadly could do nothing to help him. To their horror he collapsed and died one day before they could complete his treatment.[6]

This scenario is a typical murder theory but does not stand up to close scrutiny. To hit someone hard behind the ear is incredibly difficult; it is a most unnatural way to hit someone. The would-be assassin would have needed to hit Tutankhamun while he was lying face down, perhaps asleep. If he had been in this position, they could have continued hitting him until he was dead rather than leaving the job unfinished after a single blow. This theory also does not take account of the many other fractures to his legs and seems to be based solely on the flimsy evidence of the thinning of the bone behind the ear. This thinning of the bone could be a natural disorder caused by pressure beneath the bone or a subdural haematoma (build-up of blood), which causes a swelling on the surface of, or within the brain. The X-rays show this haematoma may have calcified, indicating that Tutankhamun survived for a couple of months after this condition developed, so the condition was not immediately fatal.[7]

Cyril Aldred did not really believe that the young king had been murdered, although he believed he did die at another's hand.[8] He cited a lesion on Tutankhamun's cheek as evidence that he died in battle, perhaps after a thrust from a spear or an arrow. This penetrated his skull, resulting in a cerebral haemorrhage, which killed him some short time later. However, there is no evidence that the wound extended into the brain.

Scientific evidence and close examination of the X-rays has disproved the murder theory. The dislodged pieces of bone in the skull, on which these theories are based, was probably caused by the rough handling of the body by Howard Carter and his team. The resin poured over the mummy by the embalmers stuck the body firmly into the coffin and the head firmly into the golden mask. The archaeologists tried to soften the resin, including using hot knives and on two occasions leaving the mummy in the hot desert sun for many hours, in temperatures up to 149 °F, which would have accelerated the deterioration of the fragile mummified tissue. High temperatures can cause mummified tissues to burst and the hot knives scraped away the tissues on his head. In their desperation to remove the mask, they eventually decapitated Tutankhamun. The torso was also cut, just above the pelvis, to remove objects in the resin beneath him. To remove his bracelets the hands were cut off at the wrist and the arms were cut at the elbow. The legs were separated at the hips and the knees and the feet were cut off during Dr Derry's examination. The feet and hands were later reattached, using resin, before being rewrapped and returned to the tomb in 1926. They placed the body in a tray of sand and crossed Tutankhamun's arms across his pelvis to hide the terrible state of the mummy from the public eye.

Further desecrations occured. Between 1926, when photographs were taken, and 1968, when further studies were made, Tutankhamun's penis and right ear had gone missing. It was believed they had been taken as souvenirs by tourists and could be languishing in private collections. Luckily, the CT scan indicated the penis is in the sand surrounding the king's body, together with other body parts, such as a thumb and vertebrae fragments. One aspect of the damage that added extra dimensions to the murder theories was the removal of his sternum (breast-bone) and rib-cage. They were initially thought to have been removed by the embalmers, perhaps due to damage caused in a crushing accident or in an attempt to ease the mummification process. However, the CT scan suggests that they were removed by Carter's team, in an attempt to remove artefacts from the chest cavity. The ribs were cut with a sharp knife and there is no evidence on the body to indicate any crushing of the chest before death. Carter's team did not mention in their reports that the ribs and sternum were missing, although they also did not record removing them. Regardless of who removed them, they remain missing.

Despite this extensive damage, it has been possible to locate body parts and identify the fragments of bone loose in the skull that were the focus of the murder theories. These bones have been identified as a piece of the top vertebra (the Atlas) and the base of the skull; if they had been dislodged before death they would have been embedded in the embalming material within the skull, whereas they were loose, indicating they were broken after mummification.[9] The 2005 CT scan displayed no evidence of a blow to the back of his head nor any other signs of foul play.

It is now generally accepted, on the basis of the CT scan, that Tutankhamun died accidentally, perhaps in a chariot accident, rather than at the hand of a murderer. The large lesion on his left cheek, seen by Aldred as evidence for death in battle, had started to heal and scab over before his death, further evidence of a survived accident. There is some disagreement among the CT scan team regarding some of the finer details of the accident. Some believe the fracture of his left thigh bone may have occurred days before his death, as there is no evidence of healing. Although this fracture would not have killed him, it would have contributed to his decline had infection set in. The fracture is at the end of the bone, a ragged rather than a sharp break, characteristic of the breaks made by Carter's team when the bones were brittle.[10] However, there is embalming material within this break on the thigh bone, indicating it may have happened before mummification. Carter also recorded that the knee cap of the left leg was loose and that there were further fractures on the right lower leg, with the knee cap wrapped into Tutankhamun's hand, again suggesting these breaks happened before embalming.[11] The rest of the CT team believe that Carter's archaeologists caused the fractures and contaminated the wound with the embalming material. They believe that if the broken limbs had led to death there would be evidence of bleeding or haematoma in the scan but none can be seen. So, it is difficult to decide if the embalming material got into the wound at the time of burial or during excavation.

Although the scan has eliminated the murder theories it has not led to unanimity on the fate of this young king. However, considering the evidence of Tutankhamun's love of hunting and charioteering, the theory of a fatal chariot accident seems believable. We do not know where he died but there are a number of possibilities. Perhaps he died at Malkata, racing down the road of Kom el 'Abd, his grandfather's chariot race track. The desert track would have been cleared but perhaps a rock was overlooked, which Tutankhamun ran over at speed, flipping the chariot and dragging him under the horses' hooves or the vehicle's wheels. Perhaps, hunting in the desert surrounding the Giza plateau, he drove too quickly and hit a rock or a dip in the sand, causing his horse to fall and upset the chariot, tossing the young king out on to the ground to be crushed by the falling chariot. The lesion on his cheek could have been caused when he landed on the ground, or by flying rocks from the wheels while riding, and may not have been a direct result of the accident.

Whatever happened, the reaction of his guards, servants, officials and family would have been shock, grief and anxiety. They would have rushed him back to the nearest palace where his physicians could try to resuscitate him and make him comfortable. This stress no doubt continued for a few days, until he finally drew his last breath. He may never have regained consciousness after the accident. If, as Brier suggests, the haematoma in Tutankhamun's skull had calcified, this would have taken a couple of months, a period when he would have been floating in and out of consciousness.[12] His doctors would have just been able to feed him and keep him alive.

As Tutankhamun did not have a male heir, the succession was unclear, which caused great anxiety both to those he left behind and to the people of Egypt. Although he named Horemheb as 'Deputy King', Ay took on the role of *sem* priest in the tomb of Tutankhamun and was clearly acting as elder son and heir. We do not know whether this was Tutankhamun's, Horemheb's or Ay's choice. The first role Ay performed as king was in the funeral of Tutankhamun, which was a traditional affair. It has been suggested that Ay arranged the funeral in secret to prevent Horemheb from returning to Thebes from Memphis to claim his place on the throne as 'Deputy King' and heir. Ay was hoping that he would be firmly on the throne by the time Horemheb arrived in Thebes.[13] This would explain the somewhat rushed and haphazard burial, with its unusual collection of childhood items and funerary goods not intended for Tutankhamun. However, keeping the death of a king secret and completing his tomb quickly would have been very difficult, if not impossible. However, it seems Ay was crowned king before Tutankhamun was buried, as in Tutankhamun's tomb, Ay is shown performing the Opening of the Mouth ceremony, with his names written in cartouches above him. How had he kept the coronation secret as well? The level of secrecy needed does not seem feasible, considering the activity involved in a royal funeral and coronation. It is more likely that, for whatever reason, Horemheb was happy to step back and allow the elderly Ay his fifteen minutes of fame on the throne of Egypt.

Tutankhamun was mummified according to tradition and we can put together the exact order of events that led to the burial of the boy king. His body would have been sent to the embalmers, where it was washed and dried before his brain was removed (through his nose) and disposed of. Then, embalming resin was placed in the skull through the nose. The embalmers did this twice: first, when he was lying on his back and then when his head was tipped or had slipped off the edge of the embalming table.[14] The two layers of resin had solidified in the top and the back of the skull at right angles to each other.[15] Some members of the 2005 CT scan team also believe that further embalming fluid was inserted via the back of the neck, as the first vertebra and the base of the skull are fractured and there is evidence of solidified fluid in this region, although other members of the team believe the fluid had dripped down to this region and that the fractures were caused by Carter's team when they removed the head to facilitate the removal of the golden mask.[16]

An incision was then made in Tutankhamun's left flank, with a flint knife, and his internal organs removed. They were preserved in natron (salt), wrapped and placed inside four miniature coffins and then into four canopic jars within his tomb. These jars, with heads representing the 'Four Sons of Horus', were designed solely for the storage of internal organs within tombs. The internal cavity was then washed out and packed with natron packages and the body laid on a bed of natron for thirty-five days, until it had completely dried out. At the end of this time, the sodden natron was removed and the slit in the left flank sealed by placing a leaf-shaped piece of gold over the opening. Then the embalmers started the wrapping, which took another thirty-five days, completing the seventy-day mummification period.

Next, each of his fingers was adorned with rings and his fingers and toes covered with golden stalls (covers), complete with nails engraved into the tips, to ensure that should the extremities decay, they would be replaced with golden ones.[17] A pair of ceremonial golden shoes was placed on his feet; these were made purely for the funeral and would not have been worn by him in life. Each of his limbs was wrapped separately, including his fingers and toes. Even his penis was wrapped in the erect position. As each of the limbs was wrapped the 'lector priest' recited prayers to turn the limb into an eternal being to aid the king's rebirth. Then the body was wrapped as one, with many layers of bandages, amidst which were secreted 143 amulets, pieces of jewellery and a golden ceremonial dagger, perhaps in recognition of his favourite pastime, hunting. The bandages were impregnated with oils and unguents to aid the preservation process. However, these oils damaged the soft tissues, rendering them very fragile; damaging them, more than preserving them. The unguents set so solidly that Howard Carter's team were unable to remove the body from the coffin without causing irreparable damage.[18]

After the many layers of bandages and jewels had been completed, Tutankhamun was covered with a large linen sheet with four bands holding it in place, then the golden mask was placed over his head. Two gold hands were placed at chest level, holding the crook and flail, and firmly stitched to the outer shroud. The body was further adorned with a gold pectoral of a human-headed *ba* bird at his throat and four bands of gold, decorated with texts from the Book of the Dead, wound around the mummy to hold the final sheets in place.

Then Ay, as the *sem* priest, carried out the 'Opening of the Mouth' ceremony and recited the appropriate incantations over the mummy. The 'Opening of the Mouth' was a very important ceremony, which enabled Tutankhamun to breath, speak, see and eat in the afterlife. The *sem* priest held a number of objects to his face, while reciting prayers and incantations. The most important of these objects was a ceremonial adze, which symbolically cut the bandages over the mouth. Then water would be sprinkled and incense burned to purify the body before it was reborn into the afterlife. Images show this ceremony being carried out while the body was vertical, so perhaps Tutankhamun was propped upright.

The mummy was then placed into the inner coffin, made of solid gold. Once his body was placed in this coffin, resin was poured over him (except over the head and feet) which gave the body an aromatic odour.[19] After the lid was placed, a floral collar was laid around the neck. Some believe this may have been left there by his grieving widow, Ankhesenamun, as a final act of love to a husband whose life was cut short so tragically. The collar was made of nine rows of flowers stitched to a semi-circular papyrus backing. Rows one, two, three and seven consisted of date palm leaves, blue/green faience rings and *withania* berries. The fifth row was made of willow and pomegranate leaves, blue water lily petals and *withania* berries. The sixth was a mixture of cornflowers, ox-tongue (*Picris radicata*), pomegranate leaves and *persea* fruits from the *Mimusops laurifolia* tree.[20] The whole effect was colourful and fragrant. A similar faience collar was discovered at Ahketaten, which bore Tutankhamun's cartouche, indicating that he would have worn something similar in life. This may be why the floral collar was made (Figure 30).

At the tomb, the golden inner coffin was placed into the second coffin and the lid lowered. Before each of the lids was closed, the

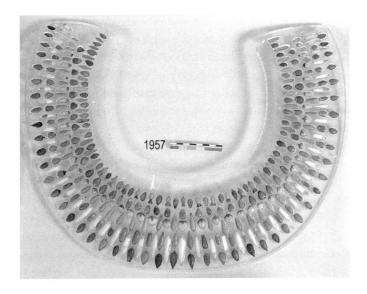

Figure 30 *Faience necklace inscribed with the cartouche of Tutankhamun from Amarna. Petrie Museum. Photograph courtesy of the Petrie Museum, UC 1957.*

coffin was wrapped in a fine linen shroud.[21] The face on the second coffin is different from that on the first and third coffins and was made in a slightly different manner. It may have been made for someone else, perhaps Smenkhkare, his brother. Two wreaths were draped over the second lid, although whether by Ankhesenamun or the funerary priests is unknown. The smallest wreath was wound around the *ureaus* on the king's brow; it was backed with papyrus and made of olive leaves and cornflowers. The leaves were laid with their top and bottom surfaces alternating, creating a green and silver pattern.[22] The second wreath on this coffin was made of four bands of floral decoration; two of olive leaves and cornflowers, one of willow leaves, water lily petals and cornflowers and one of willow, wild celery leaves and cornflowers. as the predominance of cornflowers meant the collar would have largely been blue. It was made when the leaves and flowers were fresh, as when dried they were impossible to fold and thread. These two coffins were then placed within the outer coffin.

The funerary procession, escorting the sledge dragging the body of the king, would have been an elaborate affair, accompanied by professional mourners weeping and wailing. The mummified king was dragged on a funeral bier, with the nine most influential people in the kingdom acting as pallbearers. These included the two viziers Usermont and Penthu, who are depicted as bald and wearing the traditional costume of the vizier and, bringing up the rear, Horemheb.[23] The procession of dignitaries carried tall bouquets of reeds with *persea* leaves tied to them. These were left in the tomb, propped against the wall leading to the burial chamber.[24] Behind the sled and pallbearers came a stream of servants carrying the grave goods into the tomb. Once the procession reached the tomb, the nest of coffins was placed within a red sandstone sarcophagus decorated with traditional religious images. The size of the third coffin had been miscalculated and the feet of the second coffin had to be sawn off to get the sarcophagus lid in place. The feet were thrown into the bottom of the sarcophagus, meaning this operation was carried out in the tomb, probably during the funeral. To add insult to injury, at some point the sarcophagus lid was dropped and broken. Someone made a hasty repair, plastering over the crack and painting it to disguise the damage.[25] This obviously happened before the funeral and either there was no time to carve a new lid or it was decided that the damage would never be noticed.

The sarcophagus was enclosed within four wooden and gilded shrines, too large to transport into the tomb complete; they were constructed in the tomb. The burial chamber was sealed by plastering over the entrance and the antechamber filled with the rest of the funerary goods. The last of the footprints were swept away, the tomb sealed and the entrance corridor filled with rubble. The last thing to be placed before the final sealing of the tomb was the 'embalmer's cache' of the left-over mummification materials. These were found by Theodore Davis outside KV54 in the Valley of the Kings; it is thought they were moved here after the first tomb robbery, to enable the guards to properly fill the corridor with rubble and prevent further robberies.[26]

The cache consisted of at least twelve identical whitewashed jars containing floral collars (probably worn by the mourners at the funeral) a cartonnage mask, broken pottery drinking cups, wine jars and two hand brooms. The cache was thought to be worthless – Theodore Davis handed the floral and papyrus collars found there to his dinner guests and invited them to test the strength of the 3000-year old collars by tearing them.[27] It is impossible to know how many were in the cache; sadly only three have survived intact. These collars were made of rows of flowers and leaves, including olive leaves, cornflowers, woody nightshade berries and date palm leaves, with a red trim and papyrus backing.[28] It is thought that those attending the funeral feast after the burial wore these colourful collars, which slowly would have withered and died in the harsh Egyptian heat as the feast drew to a close. The feast may even have taken place in antechamber of the tomb. The jars were filled to within a few centimetres of the top and then topped with a layer of Nile mud and white lime. There were no inscriptions; the jars are very similar to those discovered in 2006 in KV63 in the Valley of the Kings.

Close examination of the contents of the jars in KV54 revealed much about the king's mummification process. We know the embalmer's workshop was lit by saucer-shaped pottery oil lamps, as the interior was covered in a layer of soot and dregs of congealed lamp oil nestled at the bottom. The linen used for the bandages was of two types, custom-made bandages, discovered rolled up, and re-used linen from the royal household. The bandages were between 2.5 and 12.5 centimetres wide but are so fragile they cannot be unrolled. Fifty of the bandages were ripped from a larger sheet but others have a selvedge on both sides, showing they are custom made. No other ready-made bandages have ever been discovered from the eighteenth dynasty.[29] Although these linen bandages were clean, they show the fingerprints of the embalmers, who used them to wipe their hands during their messy task. Perhaps they knew they had too many. Three of the reused linen items were kerchiefs of the type worn over a shaved head to keep the dust and sun off. Two were white and one was blue; all were well-worn and had been washed so frequently that the edges were frayed. The blue one had been used as a cleaning rag and a hole had been worn all the way through.[30] It is interesting to think that these kerchiefs may have been those worn by Tutankhamun himself and after they became too tatty to wear were thrown into the old linen store to be reused.

The small mask found in one of the jars has caused some confusion, as it looks like a miniature mummy mask. It would have been placed over the mummified remains of internal organs, although strangely there is only one, rather than the customary four. The mask is 15 centimetres high, made of cartonnage and painted yellow, representative of gold. Jewellery and facial features were drawn onto the mask with blue ink. The nose of the mask was broken in antiquity, before being placed in the jar.[31] The purpose of this solitary mask remains unknown. It has been suggested it was intended for one of the babies in the tomb but was found to be too small.[32]

This cache also seems to contain the leftovers of the funerary feast. The bones included the shoulder blades of a cow, ribs of sheep or goat, geese (Brent and Bean) and ducks (teal, shovelers and gadwall). All the meat was cooked, although from the bones alone it is impossible to tell what would have accompanied the meat or what sauces it may have been served with. The cache also contained a decanter of dark-red ware, showing the food had been washed down with wine from Tutankhamun's cellar.[33] The jars were used to clean up before leaving the tomb and were considered too impure to be placed within the tomb near the body.[34]

It would appear there were eight people present at this feast. This estimate is based on the numbers of broken pottery vessels, discovered as lids and vessels and a set of eight drinking beakers.[35] The pottery seems to have been intentionally broken before being placed in the jars, perhaps so they could fit through the jar opening. The floral collars in the jars may have been worn by the guests, although there may be one missing, perhaps the one laid lovingly on the first coffin by Ankhesenamun.

The goods placed in the tomb indicate that Tutankhamun's death was totally unexpected, as many of his funerary items were not made for him. A number of items from the original Amarna burial of Smenkhkare were removed from store for the burial of the young Tutankhamun, including the second coffin, which does not bear Tutankhamun's face. However, Smenkhkare is not the only person whose funerary equipment was used; the eclectic nature of the objects suggests the stores were emptied for Tutankhamun's funeral.

The tomb itself (KV62) was hastily finished. It may have been designed not for a royal burial but rather for an official, perhaps Ay. The tomb might have been cut into the rock at the time of Tutankhamun's death and the seventy-day mummification period used to paint the tomb, although this time would have been long enough for the tomb to have been cut from scratch. However, the tomb style was royal, albeit on a small scale. The burial chamber was the only room to be decorated; there are signs that it was done quickly – the decoration is only at the top of the walls, with nothing below the dado, three-quarters of the way down the wall, other than a number of paint drips. On the ceiling are marks from the soot of the painters' lamps. They clearly did not have time to clean the tomb as well.

The palace, and Egypt, was once again in mourning a mere ten years after the death of most of the royal family at Akhetaten. The gods were clearly still not happy with their neglect during the reign of Akhenaten and were continuing to punish Egypt, killing its ruler just as he entered his political prime at eighteen years old. This premature death was a tragic end for a king who brought hope and peace to a politically and religiously unstable country. However, it is impossible to know how many of the innovations of his reign were his or whether he was merely a puppet controlled by Vizier Ay or General Horemheb. He may have been a sign of hope, but had he really had an opportunity to show his own abilities and strengths in the improvement and restoration of his beloved homeland?

Despite Tutankhamun's efforts, Egypt was still in a state of turmoil at his death. He left no heir, sowing confusion over who should succeed him. Ay took the initiative and declared himself king before the Tutankhamun was even buried. Perhaps this was an act of ambition and usurpation, or perhaps he was an astute diplomat and decided this was the best course of action to take to prevent the throne from being taken by a stranger, not of the royal family. Mourning yet another death in his family, the elderly Ay was thrown into the limelight. He had to step into the role of king and continue the work started by Tutankhamun to strengthen his drastically damaged country.

Epilogue

Tutankhamun's death left Egypt on the brink of disaster. He left no surviving son and no obvious heir, which could have led to civil war and the usurpation of the throne by any strong-willed opportunist. However, this did not happen; there was a peaceful transition of the throne to the elderly Vizier Ay, who was possibly Tutankhamun's great uncle and his only living male relative. This decision that Ay should take over the throne has raised many questions to which no satisfactory answers are available. The main one is why did Horemheb, the 'Deputy King', not ascend the throne – he was an obvious choice and closest thing to an heir.

As 'Deputy King' and military general, Horemheb was superior to Ay and could have taken the throne by force. However, Horemheb and Ay may have had an arrangement to enable a peaceful transition and both to come to the throne in turn. As the only surviving relative, father of Nefertiti, Tutankhamun's stepmother and his wife's great uncle, Ay's link to the royal family made him a legitimate heir. This decision by the powerful Horemheb to allow Ay to rule was a purely political arrangement. The major achievement of Tutankhamun's reign, supported and influenced by these two officials, was the re-establishment of the traditional religion, kingship and values. This included the succession rites. Horemheb was 'Deputy King' but he had not been officially named as heir; if he had taken the throne by force, it would not have been a surprise but could have been viewed as aggression, tainting his reign. The arrangement he made with Ay was that once crowned, Ay would officially name him as his heir, leaving no doubt as to the succession. As far as Horemheb was concerned, there was little risk in this plan; Ay was elderly and could not rule for long. Everything went according to plan. During his four-year reign Ay accompanied Horemheb to Karnak for the Opet Festival, where the oracle of Amun confirmed that Horemheb would be next in line to the throne. The oracle of Amun had not been approached since the reign of Amenhotep III, when Amun confirmed Amenhotep IV (Akhenaten) as the next king or co-regent of his father (see Chapter 1).

Ay ascended the throne in 1324 BCE, to continue Tutankhamun's restoration work. Tutankhamun's widow, Ankhesenamun, was still young, perhaps only twenty-one years old. She did not want to relinquish her position as 'King's Wife' and the power that accompanied it. Ay perhaps wanted to marry her both as a means of legitimising his right to the throne and preventing her from marrying someone else, who could perhaps use her to usurp the throne from him, but she was not keen. There were no other princes to marry (neither sons, brothers nor uncles); it is believed she wrote to the Hittite king, Supplilumas, asking him to send one of his sons to her, so she could marry him and make him king of Egypt. After much correspondence and doubt, Supplilumas agreed to send his son, Zennanza, to Egypt. Unfortunately he was murdered before he reached the Egyptian border, probably on Ay's orders. Ankhesenamun then married Ay, probably against her will, as he was much older than her. At twenty-one years old and thrice widowed, perhaps she would have preferred to be alone to grieve the loss of her half-brother and husband.

It is surprising that the letter was ever actually sent; Ay, as vizier, had access to all messages leaving the palace and was able to intercept them. Perhaps he felt that it was a harmless gesture, and that the Hittite king was certain not to believe the request and would never send his son to Egypt. I am sure he did not intend to murder the prince, as this would be detrimental to the relationship between the Egyptians and the Hittites and could result in war. If the Hittite records are to be believed, this is exactly what happened. Zennanza's murder was used by the Hittites as an excuse for war:

> But when my father gave them one of his sons, they killed him as they led him there. My father let his anger run away with him, he went to war against Egypt and attacked Egypt. He smote the foot soldiers and the charioteers of the country of Egypt. But when they brought back to Hatti Land the prisoners which they had taken, a plague broke out among the prisoners and they began to die. When they moved the prisoners to Hatti Land, the prisoners carried the plague into Hatti Land. From that day on people have been dying in the Hatti Land.[1]

Another piece of evidence for this war is a *talatat* block which was recarved and reused after the reign of Akhenaten. It depicts a Hittite charioteer, holding a squared-off shield. However, it is unknown who reused the block – Tutankhamun, Ay or Horemheb – and it may not represent this so-called battle at all. A letter from the Hittite archives also mentions the spread of the plague from the Egyptian prisoners. This plague is likely to be the same plague that saw the start of Tutankhamun's reign, causing the death of almost his entire family. It is somewhat ironic that the end of his reign was also framed by this illness.

As predicted by Horemheb, Ay died a mere four years after coming to the throne. On his death, Horemheb took his place on the throne. A military general, he was a military king; his aim was to further increase Egypt's power in the Near East. Although

Tutankhamun had improved foreign relations during his brief reign they were still somewhat short of the glory of the reign of Amenhotep III. Through the reinstatement of Egypt's power, the Egyptian military and their allies would be able to defend themselves against the growing Hittite power, as well as greatly improving the flagging economy.

Either shortly before or shortly after ascending the throne, Horemheb married his second wife, Mutnodjmet, Nefertiti's sister, as a means of legitimising his accession, through the last female link to the family of Akhenaten. Although he had been named as heir by Ay and was 'Deputy King' during Tutankhamun's reign, this marriage would eliminate any further doubt. However, although he was married twice, Horemheb had no male heirs, or at least none that survived into adulthood. The body of Mutnodjmet, believed to have been found in Horemheb's Memphite tomb, shows she possibly died in childbirth; her pelvis suggests that she had given birth many times but she seems to have either borne only daughters or sons that had died in infancy.

To prevent confusion following his death, Horemheb named his heir during his reign; General Prameses. He hailed from the Delta region and had no connections with the Amarna period. He had a son, ensuring that the new royal line would continue. Prameses was first promoted to vizier and then to 'Deputy King'. On Horemheb's death, he became king, naming himself Ramses (I). Historians like to think of him as the first king of the nineteenth dynasty and of the line of Ramesside kings, although it was really Horemheb who started the changes that were the beginning of a new era. The Ramesside family did not forget the opportunity that Horemheb gave to Ramses I; his Memphite tomb became an important shrine for them, with additions set up by Ramses II, the grandson of Ramses I.

As another way of legitimising his rule and separating himself from the Amarna kings, Horemheb eliminated all traces of them.

Once Mutnodjmet died and the final link had been severed, Horemheb started a campaign against Akhenaten, Smenkhkare, Tutankhamun and Ay, destroying their monuments and erasing them from history. He counted his regnal years from the end of the reign of Amenhotep III, as if the four kings in between had never existed. Luckily, Horemheb's men ignored Tutankhamun's tomb; it has been suggested that the entrance had been lost. However, many people knew the location of the tomb, including the Overseer, Maya and Horemheb himself, as they had attended the funeral. It is more likely that Horemheb decided to leave the tomb; it was out of sight and therefore out of mind and could not damage his reign through association.

However, despite the tomb's apparent disappearance, there were at least two robberies in antiquity. The first robbery happened shortly after the burial, when the newly-covered entrance was still visible on the landscape; the second robbery shortly afterwards, when the tomb had been sealed by the priests and Valley Guards. The corridor to the tomb had been filled with rubble before the doorway was sealed: the robbers created a small crawl-space in the upper left-hand corner, which allowed one person through at a time. In this dark, hot and dusty space, the robbers passed rock and debris back through the hole to their waiting companions for up to eight hours. When the robbers reached the second doorway, it was easy to break through and enter the tomb. They were selective in the goods they took as they needed to take objects that could be easily sold, with no questions being asked about their origins. The first robbers took gold and jewellery, which could be melted down and sold on. The second robbers took the oils and unguents; this time, they were equipped with goatskins, indicating perhaps the robberies were carried out by the same people.

In the torches' dim light it would be difficult to tell solid gold from gilded wood, so to ease their search they threw the caskets into the centre of the antechamber, emptying them so they could search them in the brightest light. It is difficult to identify everything that was taken during the robberies, although the labels on the empty caskets indicate what is missing. A bundle of solid gold rings knotted into a scarf, which the thief had dropped on the way out, was discovered; perhaps the robbers had been disturbed by the Valley Guards. After the robbers had thoroughly searched the antechamber, they broke into the annexe and emptied the precious oils into their goatskins. These oils which have been sold in or around Thebes. In his rush to empty the oils, as he scraped the dregs from the bottom, one of the robbers left his fingerprint in the oil on the inside of the jar. If the ancients had had the ability to match fingerprints, the robbers would have been caught. A second robber left his footprints on a white wooden box, which he scrambled over in his search for further treasure. From the annexe, the robbers made their way through to the burial chamber and into the treasury, guarded by Anubis, seated on his shrine. Many pieces of jewellery were taken, although how much and what we will probably never know. A large amount of gold inlaid jewellery was left in the treasury; it is thought the robbers may have been disturbed and left the tomb.

The morning after the first robbery, the Valley Guards noticed the robbers' hole and entered the tomb via the same route. They evaluated the damage and attempted to tidy the tomb into some sort of order, picking up the scattered objects and hurriedly placing them in the open caskets. The scarf with the rings was thrown unceremoniously into one of the caskets, amongst other objects. They were obviously working quickly and many items ended up in the wrong boxes. They then resealed the doors and filled the tunnel with rubble. The robbers do not seem to have been caught, hence they returned a second time and were again able to escape. However, the Valley guards obviously did a good job of covering the tomb after the second robbery, as it remained intact throughout the destruction of Horemheb and the robberies of the later Egyptian periods, which saw the destruction of many of the Valley tombs. Tutankhamun's tomb remained virtually intact, one of very few in the Valley of the Kings; Horemheb did not succeed in eliminating this young boy from the annals of history.

Notes and references

Introduction

1. Redford D. 1984: *Akhenaten, the heretic king.* Princeton. Princeton University Press. p. 215.
2. Weigall A. 1923: 'The Malevolence of Ancient Egyptian Spirits' in Frayling C. 1992: *The Face of Tutankhamun.* London. Faber and Faber. p. 232.
3. Nelson M.R. 2002: 'The Mummy's curse: historical cohort study' in *BMJ* 325, pp. 1482–5. p. 1484.
4. Desroches-Noblecourt C. 1971: *Tutankhamun.* Harmondsworth. Penguin. p. 20.
5. Nelson 2002: p. 1482.
6. Frayling C. 1992: *The Face of Tutankhamun.* London. Faber and Faber. p. 212.
7. Hawass Z. 2005a: *Tutankhamun Facial Reconstruction.* Cairo. Press Release.

Chapter 1 Setting the scene

1. Fletcher J. 2000: *Chronicle of a Pharaoh: the intimate life of Amenhotep III.* Oxford. Oxford University Press. p. 50.
2. Fletcher 2000: p. 146
3. Shaw I. 2000: 'Egypt and the Outside World' in Shaw I. (ed.) *The Oxford History of Ancient Egypt.* Oxford. Oxford University Press. p. 326.

4. Clayton P. 1994: *Chronicle of the Pharaohs*. London. Thames and Hudson. p. 117.

5. El Mahdy C. 1999: *Tutankhamun: The life and death of a Boy King*. London. Headline. p. 224.

6. El Mahdy 1999: p. 170

7. El Mahdy 1999: p. 240

8. Montserrat D. 2000: *Akhenaten; History, Fantasy and Ancient Egypt*. London. Routledge. p. 45.

9. Desroches-Noblecourt 1971: p. 93

10. Fairman H.W. 1938: 'Preliminary report on the Excavations at Sesebi, Northern Province, Anglo-Egyptian Sudan 1937–8' in *Journal of Egyptian Archaeology* 24, pp. 151–6.

11. Blackman A.M. 1937: 'Preliminary report on the Excavations at Sesebi, Northern Province, Anglo-Egyptian Sudan 1936–7' in *Journal of Egyptian Archaeology* 23, pp. 145–51.

12. Blackman 1937: p. 146

13. Blackman 1937: p. 147

14. Blackman 1937: p. 148

15. Winfield Smith R. 1976: in *The Akhenaten Temple Project Vol I*. Warminster. Aris and Phillips. p. 42.

16. Winfield Smith 1976: p. 23

17. Redford D. 1976: in *The Akhenaten Temple Project Vol I*.

18. Blackman 1937: p. 146

19. El Mahdy 1999: p. 189

Chapter 2 Akhetaten: a new beginning

1. Reeves N. 2005: *Akhetaten: Egypt's False Prophet*. London. Thames and Hudson. pp. 116–17.

2. Reeves 2005: p. 109

3. Desroches-Noblecourt 1971: p. 97

4. Reeves 2005: p. 110

5. Kemp B.J. 1983: 'Tell el 'Amarna' in Smith H.S. & Hall R. (eds.) *Ancient Centres of Egyptian Civilisation*. London. Impads. pp. 57–72.

6. Reeves 2005: p. 103

7. El Mahdy 1999: pp. 190–1

8. Desroches-Noblecourt 1971: p. 107

9. Reeves 2005: p. 110

10. Reeves 2005: p. 110

11. Reeves 2005: p. 111

12. Kemp 1991: *Anatomy of a Civilisation*. London. Routledge. p. 276.

13. Reeves 2005: p. 119

14. Kemp 1991: p. 276

15. Reeves 2005: p. 120

16. Desroches-Noblecourt 1971: p. 120

17. Desroches-Noblecourt 1971: p. 117

18. Samson J. 1985: *Nefertiti and Cleopatra*. London. Rubicon Press. p. 48.

19. Desroches-Noblecourt 1971: p. 120

20. Samson 1985: p. 40

21. Desroches-Noblecourt 1971: p. 105

22. Samson 1985: pp. 96–7

Chapter 3   A king is born

1. KV (King's Valley) is the referencing system used to number the tombs in the Valley of the Kings. The numbers refer to the order in which they were discovered. KV62 was the 62nd tomb discovered in the Valley of the Kings and belongs to Tutankhamun.

2. van Djik J. & Eaton-Krauss M. 1985: 'Tutankhamun at Memphis' in *MDAIK* 42, pp. 35–41.

3. Fairman H.W. 1972: 'Tutankhamun and the end of the eighteenth dynasty' in *Antiquity* 46, pp. 15–18

4. Robins G. 1991: 'The Mother of Tutankhamun' in *Discussions in Egyptology* 20, pp. 71–3

5. Robins 1991: p. 72

6. This is a masonry block introduced by Akhenaten. The name *talatat* comes from the Arabic for three, and is in reference to the block being a hand high, a hand wide and a hand deep.

7. Ray J. 1975: 'The Parentage of Tutankhamun' in *Antiquity* 49, pp. 45–7.

8. Robins G. 1992: 'The Mother of Tutankhamun' in *Discussions in Egyptology* 22, pp. 25–7.

9. Robins 1992: pp. 25–7

10. El Mahdy 1999: p. 242

11. Fairman 1972: p. 17

12. Zivie A. 1998: 'The Tomb of the Lady Maia, wet-nurse of Tutankhamun' in *Egyptian Archaeology* 13, pp. 7–8.

13. Zivie 1998: p. 7

14. Reeves N. 1990: *The Complete Tutankhamun*. London. Thames and Hudson. p. 187.

15. Eaton-Krauss M. 1995: 'Notes on some New Kingdom stools with Bulls' Legs and Tutankhamun's 'Feeding Chair'' in *Divitae Aegypti: Koptologische und Verwandte Studeien zu ehren von Martin Krause.* Wiesbaden. Dr Ludwig Reichert Verlag. pp. 85–92.

16. Desroches-Noblecourt 1971: p. 199

17. Manniche L. 1976: *Musical Instruments from the Tomb of Tu'tankhamun.* Oxford. Griffith Institute. pp. 3–4.

18. Manniche 1976: pp. 3–4

19. Manniche 1976: pp. 5–6

20. Manniche 1976: pp. 5–6

21. Reeves 1990: pp. 168–9

22. Kemp 1991: p. 222

23. Reeves 1990: p. 169

24. Hepper N. 1990: *Pharaoh's Flowers: The botanical treasures of Tutankhamun.* London. HMSO Publication Centre. p. 29.

25. Larson J.A. 1991: 'The Tutankhamun Astronomical Instrument' in *Amarna Letters* 1, pp. 77–83.

26. Larson 1991: p. 81

27. Larson 1991: p. 82

28. Littauer M.A. & Crouwell J.H. 1985: *Chariots and Related Equipment from the Tomb of Tut'ankhamun.* Oxford. Griffith Institute.

29. Hepper 1990: p. 30

30. Hepper 1990: p. 44

31. Lehner M. 1991: *Archaeology of an Image: The Great Sphinx of Giza.* Unpublished PhD thesis. Yale University. pp. 54–7.

32. Kemp 1991: p. 219

33. Kemp B. 1973: 'A Building of Amenophis III at Kom El-'Abd' in *Journal of Egyptian Archaeology* 63, pp. 71–82.

34. Kemp 1973: pp. 77–8

35. Kemp 1973: pp. 77–8
36. David R. 1986: *The Pyramid Builders of Ancient Egypt.* London. Guild Publishing. p. 90.
37. El Mahdy 1999: p. 295
38. Tait W.J. 1982: *Game Boxes and Accessories from the Tomb of Tut'ankhamun.* Oxford. Griffith Institute. p. 42.
39. Tait 1982: p. 43
40. Tait 1982: p. 17
41. Desroches-Noblecourt 1971: p. 123
42. El Mahdy 1999: p. 53
43. El Mahdy 1999: p. 295
44. Desroches-Noblecourt 1971: p. 125
45. Ray J. 1975: 'The Parentage of Tutankhamun' in *Antiquity* 49, pp. 45–7.
46. El Mahdy 1999: p. 140
47. Panagiotakopulu E. 2004: 'Pharaonic Egypt and the origins of plague' in *Journal of Biogeography* 31, pp. 269–75.
48. Interview with Barry Kemp on www.archaeology.org/online/interviews/kemp.html

Chapter 4 Ascent to the throne

1. Desroches-Noblecourt 1971: p. 132
2. Leek F.F. 1972: *The Human Remains from the tomb of Tut'ankhamun.* Oxford. Griffith Institute. p. 22.
3. Harrison R.G. et al. 1979: 'A Mummified Foetus from the Tomb of Tutankhamun' in *Antiquity* 53, pp. 9–21.
4. Brier B. 1999: *The Murder of Tutankhamun.* New York. Berkley Books. pp. 160–1.
5. Harrison 1979: p. 21
6. El Mahdy 1999: p. 137
7. Desroches-Noblecourt 1971: p. 154
8. Desroches-Noblecourt 1971: p. 142
9. Hepper 1990: p. 10
10. Vartavan C. de 2002: *Hidden fields of Tutankhamun: from identification to interpretation of newly discovered plant material from the Pharaoh's grave.* London. Triade Exploration Ltd. p. 173.

11. A tree that grows in very dry environments; parts of the tree were used for perfume, dyes and medicine.

12. El Mahdy 1999: pp. 43–4

13. Fletcher J. 2005: *The Search for Nefertiti*. London. Hodder and Stoughton.

14. Hawass Z. 2005b: 'King Tut Returns' in *KMT* vol. 16, no. 2, pp. 20–37.

15. El Mahdy 1999: p. 251

16. Černy J. 1965: *Hieratic Inscriptions from the tomb of Tutankhamun*. Oxford. Griffith Institute. pp. 17–18.

17. Černy 1965: p. 18

18. Boodle L.A. 1933: Appendix 2 in Vartavan C. de 2002 (ed.) *Hidden fields of Tutankhamun: from identification to interpretation of newly discovered plant material from the Pharaoh's grave*. London. Triade Exploration Ltd. pp. 190–4.

19. Hepper 1990: p. 54

20. Hepper 1990: p. 52

21. Hepper 1990: p. 50

22. Guasch-Jané M.R. et al. 2006: 'The origin of the Ancient Egyptian Drink *Shedeh* revealed using LC/MS/MS' in *Journal of Archaeological Science*, pp. 98–101.

23. Lesko L. 1977: *King Tut's Wine Cellar*. Albany. Albany Press. Appendix.

24. Lesko 1977: p. 17

25. Lesko 1977: p. 19

26. Lesko 1977: p. 20

27. Lesko 1977: p. 14

28. Lesko 1977: p. 29

29. Lesko 1977: p. 35

30. Guasch-Jané 2006: p. 99

31. Guasch-Jané 2006: p. 98

32. Guasch-Jané 2006: pp. 98–101

33. Guasch-Jané 2006: p. 100

34. Černy 1965: pp. 9–10

35. Černy 1965: pp. 9–10

36. Leek 1972: p. 12

37. Hepper 1990: p. 19
38. Černy 1965: p. 13
39. Černy 1965: p. 14

Chapter 5   Diplomat and warrior

1. Dodson A. & Hilton D. 2004: *The Complete Royal Families of Ancient Egypt*. London. Thames and Hudson. p. 154.

2. Schaden O. 1977: *The God's Father Ay*. London. University Microfilms International. p. 66.

3. Schaden 1977: p. 138

4. Desroches-Noblecourt 1971: p. 134

5. El Mahdy 1999: p. 243

6. Habachi L. 1979: 'Unknown or little-known monuments of Tutankhamun and of his Viziers' in Ruffle J., Gabella G. and Kitchen K. (eds.) *Glimpses of Ancient Egyptian Studies in Honour of H.W. Fairman*. Warminster. Aris and Phillips. pp. 32–41.

7. El Mahdy 1999: pp. 317–19

8. Desroches-Noblecourt 1971: p. 139

9. Amer A. 1984: 'Tutankhamun's decree for the Chief Treasurer Maya' in *RdE* 35, pp. 17–20.

10. Amer 1984: p. 20

11. Eaton-Krauss M. 1988: 'Tutankhamun at Karnak' in *MDAIK* 44, pp. 1–11.

12. Schaden 1977: pp. 154–7

13. Eaton-Krauss 1988: p. 4

14. Schaden 1977: pp. 190–1

15. Bell L. 1985: 'Aspects of the Cult of the Deified Tutankhamun' in *Mélanges Gamal Eddin Mokhtar. Publié sous la direction de Paule Posener-Kriéger*. Cairo. Institut Français d'Archéologie Orientale. pp. 31–59.

16. Bell 1985: p. 38

17. Strudwick N. & Strudwick H. 1999: *Thebes in Egypt*. London. British Museum Press. p. 84

18. Habachi 1979: p. 35

19. Forbes D.C. 2005: 'Beyond the Tomb: the historical Tutankhamun' in *KMT* vol. 16, no. 2, pp. 38–50.

20. van Dijk & Eaton-Krauss 1986: p. 35

21. Desroches-Noblecourt 1971: p. 161

22. Bell 1985: p. 34

23. Habachi 1979: p. 35

24. Desroches-Noblecourt 1971: p. 154

25. Booth C. 2005: *The Role of Foreigners in Ancient Egypt: A Study of Non-stereotypical Artistic Representations.* Oxford. British Archaeological Reports International.

26. Desroches-Noblecourt 1971: p. 157

27. Johnson. W.R. 1992: *An Asiatic Battle Scene of Tutankhamun from Thebes: A late Amarna Antecedent of the Ramesside Battle Narrative.* Unpublished PhD Thesis. University of Chicago. p. 12, & Eaton-Krauss 1988: p. 7.

28. Manniche 1976: pp. 7–8

29. Manniche 1976: pp. 9–11

30. Manniche 1976: p. 13

31. Manniche 1976: p. 11

32. Manniche 1976: p. 13

33. James T.G.H. 1991: *Howard Carter: the path to Tutankhamun.* London. Kegan Paul International. p. 389.

34. Manniche 1976: p. 13

35. Easton-Krauss 1988: p. 7

36. Johnson 1992: p. 109

Chapter 6   The decade draws to a close

1. Fairman 1972: p. 16

2. Desroches-Noblecourt 1971: p. 158

3. Leek 1972: p. 14

4. Harrison R.G & Abdalla A.B. 1972: 'The remains of Tutankhamun' in *Antiquity* XLVI, pp. 8–18.

5. Leek 1972: p. 16

6. El Mahdy 1999: p. 302

7. Brier 1999: p. 173

8. Aldred C. 1968: *Akhenaten; Pharaoh of Egypt.* London. Abacus. p. 183

9. Hawass 2005b: p. 34

10. Hawass Z. 2005c: *Tutankhamun CT Scan*. Cairo. Press Release.

11. Hawass 2005b: p. 34

12. Brier 1999: p. 173

13. El Mahdy 1999: p. 308

14. Brier 1999: p. 167

15. Leek 1972: p. 17

16. Hawass 2005c.

17. Leek 1972: p. 14

18. Desroches-Noblecourt 1971: pp. 163–4

19. Hepper 1990: p. 19

20. Hepper 1990: p. 9

21. Desroches-Noblecourt 1971: p. 179

22. Hepper 1990: p. 9

23. Habachi 1979: p. 40

24. Hepper 1990: p. 9

25. Desroches-Noblecourt 1971: p. 179

26. Allen 2000: p. 24

27. Winlock H.E. 1941: *Materials used at the Embalming of King Tūt-
    'ankh-amūn*. New York. Arno Press. p. 6.

28. Winlock 1941: p. 17, Hepper p. 10

29. Winlock 1941: p. 10

30. Winlock 1941: p. 10

31. Winlock 1941: p. 12

32. Allen 2000: p. 26

33. Lesko 1977: p. 46

34. Winlock 1941: p. 7

35. Allen 2000: p. 28

Epilogue

1. Brier 1999: p. 181

INDEX